INTERMEDIATE LOAN

THIS ITEM MAY BE BORROWED FOR

ONE WEEK ONLY

**INTERMEDIATE LOANS ARE IN HEAVY DEMAND,
PLEASE RETURN OR RENEW**

To renew, telephone:
01243 816089 (Bishop Otter)
01243 812099 (Bognor Regis)

2 1 NOV 2003
1 8 MAR 2006

1 8 APR 2006

0 6 NOV 2006

19. JAN 09.

the self-evaluation guidelines, 'How Good is Our School?'

UNIVERSITY COLLEGE CHICHESTER LIBRARIES

AUTHOR:

WS 2209889 5

TITLE:

CLASS NO:
371.207 MAC

DATE:
9/03

SUBJECT: TES

What's in it for schools?

Edited by Kate Myers and John MacBeath

Inspection: What's in it for schools?

James Learmonth

Leadership: What's in it for schools?

Thomas J. Sergiovanni

Self-evaluation: What's in it for schools?

John MacBeath and Archie McGlynn

Self-evaluation

What's in it for schools?

**John MacBeath
and Archie McGlynn**

London & New York

First published 2002 by RoutledgeFalmer
11 New Fetter Lane, London EC4P 4EE

Simultaneously published in the USA and Canada
by RoutledgeFalmer
29 West 35th Street, New York, NY 10001

RoutledgeFalmer is an imprint of the Taylor & Francis Group

© 2002 John MacBeath and Archie McGlynn

Typeset in Baskerville by
Keystroke, Jacaranda Lodge, Wolverhampton
Printed and bound in Great Britain by
TJ International Ltd, Padstow, Cornwall

All rights reserved. No part of this book may be reprinted or reproduced
or utilised in any form or by any electronic, mechanical, or other means,
now known or hereafter invented, including photocopying and
recording, or in any information storage or retrieval system, without
permission in writing from the publishers.

British Library Cataloguing in Publication Data
A catalogue record for this book is available from the British Library

Library of Congress Cataloging in Publication Data
A catalog record for this title has been requested.

ISBN 0–415–27741–8 (hbk)
ISBN 0–415–27742–6 (pbk)

Contents

Figures

Tables

Series Editors' preface

Kate Myers and John MacBeath

Series introduction

There is a concerted move to raise standards in the public education system. The aim is laudable. Few people would disagree with it. However, there is no clear agreement about what we mean by 'standards'. Do we mean attainment or achievement more broadly defined, for example, and how we are to raise whatever it is we agree needs raising?

At the same time, there appears to be an increasing trend towards approaching changes in education through a controlling, rational and technical framework. This framework tends to concentrate on educational content and delivery and ignores the human resource perspective and the complexity of how human beings live, work and interact with one another. It overemphasizes linearity and pays insufficient attention to how people respond to change and either support or subvert it.

Recent government initiatives, including the National Curriculum, OfSTED school and LEA inspections, assessment procedures, league tables, target-setting, literacy and numeracy hours, and performance management have endorsed this framework. On occasions this has been less to do with the content of 'reforms' than the process of implementation – that is, doing it 'to' rather than 'with' the teaching profession. Teachers are frequently treated as the problem rather than part of the solution, with the consequence that many feel disillusioned, demoralised and disempowered. Critics of this *top-down* approach are often seen as lacking rigour, complacent about standards, and uninterested in raising achievement.

We wanted to edit this series because we believe that you can be passionate about public education, about raising achievement, about ensuring that all pupils are entitled to the best possible education that society is able to provide – whatever their race, sex or class. We also believe that achieving this is not a simple matter of common sense or of the appliance of science – it is more complex than that. Most of all, we see the teaching profession as an important part of the solution to finding ways through these complexities.

What's in it for schools? is a series that will make educational policy issues relevant to practitioners. Each book in the series focuses on a major educational issue and raises key questions, such as:

- can inspection be beneficial to schools?
- how can assessment procedures help pupils learn?
- how can school self-evaluation improve teaching and learning?
- what impact does leadership in the school have in the classroom?
- how can school improvement become classroom improvement?

The books are grounded in sound theory, recent research evidence and best practice, and aim to:

- help you to make meaning personally and professionally from knowledge in a given field;
- help you to seek out practical applications of an area of knowledge for classrooms and schools;
- help those of you who want to research the field in greater depth, by providing key sources with accessible summaries and recommendations.

In addition, each chapter ends with a series of questions for reflection or further discussion, enabling schools to use the books as a resource for whole-school staff development.

We hope that the books in this series will show you that there are ways of raising achievement that can take account of how schools grow and develop and how teachers work and interact with one another. *What's in it for schools?* – a great deal, we think!

1 Why evaluate schools?

Why evaluate schools? Why not leave them alone to do what they do best, to get on with the business of teaching and learning?

The answer is simple. There is no alternative. For as long as we have had schools we have evaluated them. We have not always done it well or systematically. It has often been intuitive, off the cuff, a matter of hearsay and reputation. And what have often been widely regarded as good schools have benefited from mythology and mystique. Evaluating the quality of schools is not just the researcher's province. It has always been an element in people's everyday vocabulary. Whatever the nature of their judgements, the quality of schools has for many years been a matter of concern to most parents, some of whom put their child's name down for 'a good school' even before their child is born. Virtually every parent wants his or her child to have 'a good education' and that is often equated with sending him or her to a 'good' school.

But what lies beneath the comment 'It's a good school'? What meanings are attached to that judgement, and what differing forms do meanings take when pronounced by a politician, a journalist, an inspector, a pupil, a researcher, or a parent recommending their own child's school to a neighbour? And what is the difference between a 'good' school and an 'effective' one?

How good is effectiveness?

The term 'effective' has passed imperceptibly into our everyday vocabulary and into policy dialogue. It is often used synonymously with 'good', so concealing a multitude of possible meanings. For the purist researcher, effectiveness is a measurement of progress over and above what might have been predicted from pupils' background characteristics and prior attainment. That is what is commonly referred to as the 'added value' which is the mark of an effective school as against a 'good' one. By this definition, a school is effective when it surpasses the predictions about the future success of its pupils. The 'value' that is added is normally a reference to extra unpredicted attainment that exceeded the forecast of prior attainment or baseline measurement. It is what appears 'above the line' on any graph which compares attainment at two points in time (as in Figure 1.1.).

A decade or so ago teachers in the United Kingdom might have been baffled by such statistical wizardry, but third-millennium schools have had to familiarise themselves with this way of thinking about their work and this way of measuring their success. However, most teachers, most researchers and policy-makers too, regard such a measure of success as only partial and potentially misleading. It is hard to see how any school could be called effective without broader measures of achievement such as improved attitudes, motivation, raised esteem and difficult-to-measure skills such as learning to learn. The more we stretch the definition of effectiveness, however, the more difficult it becomes to see the difference

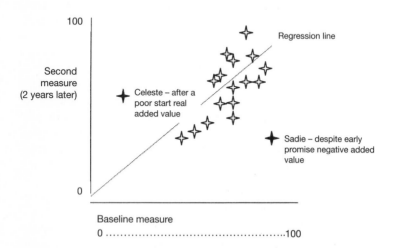

Figure 1.1 Illustrating value-added attainment

between the 'good' and the 'effective', and it is difficult to see how an effective school could not be good and a good school not effective.

Good schools and effective schools are, ultimately, a matter of perspective. They depend on the criteria we use for our judgement, however implicit or explicit these criteria are. All judgements are made in a context, within a culture and within a linguistic convention. All our evaluations subsume clusters of value judgements, beliefs and opinions. Sometimes these are so deeply embedded in our thinking and discourse that they are not open to question. Some value judgements are taken as so fundamental to human life and well-being that they are beyond question. For example, no one is prepared to contest that learning is a good thing, that age is a significant factor in deciding what children should and shouldn't know, or that children's behaviour and beliefs should be shaped by adults. In other words, there is a moral base on which school education is allowed to rest and that moral base is a virtually universal one.

What is good about good schools?

Going beyond these unquestioned taken-as-read value judgements there is a fairly solid core of agreement on what is good about schools. Irrespective of culture we prefer orderly to disorderly schools, well-managed to badly-managed schools, schools in which pupils show progress over time, schools in which teachers monitor and assess how well their pupils are doing. We believe that parents are necessary and valued co-educators and that children learn best when there is some form of bridge between home and school learning. We believe that learning has a social dimension and that it is good for children to cooperate with and learn from one another.

These are generally undisputed characteristics, or benchmarks, of good schools. They are ones which we continually monitor and measure in the day-to-day life of schools and classrooms. We do this mostly in a subjective or intuitive fashion, only becoming concerned when these basic tenets are breached in some way. Our consensus on common values might progress quite a distance before we begin to diverge in our judgements, but we sooner or later do reach a point where our opinions begin to become more contested. These differences become progressively more acute across different national contexts, cultures and ethnic languages.

Yet even beneath a common language and a common national culture lie some quite different understandings of the emphasis and priority that ought to be given to some values as against others. We reach a point too where we begin to dissect the common language and discover that it sometimes conceals more than it reveals.

Virtually everyone wants schools in which children respect their teachers, but what does 'respect' mean? Everyone believes that pupils should behave well, but can they agree on what constitutes 'good' behaviour? Order is inherently preferable to disorder, but how do we distinguish one from the other? Is someone's disorder another's order? Highly interactive noisy classrooms may be underpinned by order which is not apparent at first sight and a highly ordered classroom may conceal beneath its surface slow educational death.

What may have appeared at first sight to be simple and common-sensical turns out to be so complex that it is tempting is to abandon systematic evaluation and trust to the sound professional judgement of each individual teacher or headteacher. However, it is the very complexity of what makes for good, and less good, schools that makes evaluation compelling, significant and worth pursuing.

The 'pursuing' of evaluation has, historically, come from three main directions:

- from the top down, driven by political pressures, nationally and internationally, to assure quality and deliver value for money;
- from the bottom up, stimulated by schools seeking strategies and tools for self-improvement;
- from sideways on, from researchers and commentators, in particular school effectiveness research which has, over three decades, pursued inquiry into what makes schools effective and what it is that helps schools improve.

These three strands of development are virtually impossible to disentangle in simple cause-and-effect terms. Researchers could not have produced their findings without the insights and collaboration of teachers. Policy-makers relied on researchers to lend authority to their pronouncements. Research and policy fed back into school and classroom practice. And, as in the natural order of things, the implicit becomes gradually more explicit, the informal becomes formal and evaluation is discovered, and rediscovered, from generation to generation.

The Germans have a word, '*Zeitgeist*', to describe a climate of ideas whose time has come. The need for better, more systematic, evaluation of schools is a third millennium global zeitgeist. It finds a common meeting ground of schools and authorities, policy-makers and politicians, researchers and academics. There is an emerging consensus among these various groups and across nations that we want to get better at evaluation because it is good for pupils, for parents and for teachers because without it what is learned is simply a matter of hunch, guesswork and opinion.

Beneath this happy consensus, however, lie some deeply contested issues. Evaluation is a good thing, but who should do it? We all want better evaluation, but what should be evaluated? Evaluation is necessary, but when and how should it be carried out? Evaluation is beneficial, but who is it for?

Who should evaluate?

A decade or so ago we might have answered this with a simple retort – Her Majesty's Inspectors. Or perhaps, we might have entrusted this to local education authority inspectors or advisers. In 2002 a more common answer to the question would be: 'Schools themselves'. There does, however, appear to be an emerging consensus that the most satisfactory answer to the question is both. Both internal and external evaluation have complementary roles to play. (This is the theme we explore in chapter 2.)

What should we evaluate?

Evaluating schools has been a major thrust of policy in the last two decades in the UK. It has drawn heavily on the work of school-effectiveness researchers and their three-decade-long pursuit of the question 'What makes an effective school?' with assumptions built into that question that have been increasingly challenged by others from different fields of inquiry (see, for example, Thrupp, 1999).

Effectiveness research has taken the school as the unit of analysis, working on the assumption that a school as an entity makes a critical difference, and that going to school A as against school B is a prime determinant of life chances. Inspection and reporting in all UK countries has similarly taken the school as the unit of analysis and reported publicly on the quality of the school, its ethos, leadership, shared culture of learning and teaching. Evaluation at whole-school level is less taken for granted in other cultures, however. Countries such as France and Belgium have tended to focus inspection on individual classrooms and individual teachers. In many German states, Swiss cantons or Danish communes, teachers have enjoyed a considerable measure of individual autonomy, neither seeing the need to know what other teachers were doing in their classrooms nor accepting the necessity of senior management observing or evaluating the quality of their teaching.

While the school effect has been reported in highly optimistic terms – 'Schools can make a difference' (Brookover et al., 1979), 'School matters' (Rutter, Mortimore et al., 1979) – researchers have come progressively to the recognition that schools make less of a difference than teachers. So in recent years effectiveness researchers have turned their attention much more to the internal characteristics of schools, to departments and classrooms as the focal point for what differentiates success from failure. Unsurprising as such a refocusing might be, the implications are far-reaching. It means that if we are to get a true and faithful measure of effectiveness our primary concern has to be with what happens in individual classrooms, with individual teachers and with individual learners.

This refocusing more on what happens in classrooms should not, however, ignore the wider focus on school culture. It is not a matter of either or: school or classroom, management or teachers, teaching or learning. Measuring effectiveness means sharpening our thinking as to where we should give most attention and invest our energies at any given time and in light of the priorities we pursue. And as we get better at it we recognize that in good schools the boundaries between different levels become so blurred that they defy even the most inventive of statistical techniques.

Research and school experience point towards three main levels, which may be illustrated as in Figure 1.2.

At the centre of our model we have to put pupil learning, because this is unarguably the most central and significant purpose of school education. At the second level is culture, that is the climate and conditions which not only enable pupil learning to flourish but also sustain staff learning. The third level is leadership, that is the direction and driving force which creates and maintains the culture. Taken together these three

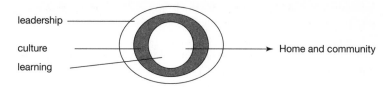

Figure 1.2 Circles of evaluation

points of focus provide the essential constituents of the school as a learning community.

There is, however, a critical missing ingredient, indicated by the arrow which points out from the school to the home and community. None of what takes place at any of these three levels can be evaluated in any meaningful sense without reference to the wider context in which they operate. Leadership must be outward-looking and responsive to the needs and expectations of both the local and the wider community. Culture is not merely something fabricated within the school walls but is brought in by pupils and teachers, a product of past histories and future hopes. Learning is as much a home and community matter as a school matter, and how children learn outside school should be as critical a focus of evaluation as what they learn inside classrooms.

In deciding *what* to evaluate there is an irresistible temptation to measure what is easiest and most accessible to measurement. Measurement of pupil attainment is unambiguously concrete and appealing because over a century and more we have honed the instruments for assessing attainment and for a century and more these pupil-attainment measures have provided benchmarks for teachers and those who had an interest in monitoring and comparing teacher effectiveness.

Numbers of words correctly spelt, percentage of correct answers on an arithmetic test, words decoded correctly on a reading test, or terms translated correctly from French to English provide fairly unambiguous performance measures. This process is normally described as 'assessment' because it measures individual attainment, but these measures have served evaluation purposes too because they provide evidence on the performance of a group – an ethnic group, boys and girls, a class, a school, an authority or a nation. So, we have volumes of data on the attainment of boys as against girls, the underperformance of certain ethnic groups and, in addition, large-scale international studies such as the Third

International Mathematics and Science Study (TIMSS) which aggregates pupil-attainment scores to national level in order to compare how different countries perform.

In the process evaluation has become so clearly associated with assessment that the terms now tend to be used interchangeably. The distinction is, however, critical. If the evaluation of national, school or teacher effects rests on assessment of pupil performance we must be clear about the assumptions and limitations of that view.

Evaluation and assessment – making the distinction

The distinction between assessment and evaluation may be illustrated by taking the example of the individual pupil. A pupil may be asked to assess for himself a recently completed piece of work, perhaps giving it a grade or applying a set of given criteria. In this way the pupil shares with the teacher in the assessment process. However, if the pupil is asked to engage in evaluation it requires taking a further step back, moving outside the situation, addressing questions such as these:

- Was the experience worthwhile?
- Were the criteria for assessment the right ones?
- What did I learn from that process?
- What might I do next time to improve?
- How am I developing as an effective learner?

Evaluation of a school should pursue equally testing questions. It should cast its net wider than easy-to-measure performance. It should reflect on how the school learns and what it needs to do to improve. It should be concerned with critical issues of consultation and decision-making which may include or exclude, affirm or undermine, the morale of staff. It should be concerned with the hopes and aspirations of pupils and their satisfaction as to how well those hopes and aspirations have been met. It should concern itself with the satisfaction of teachers, personal and professional, the quality of relationships, the breadth of opportunities and the equality of access to them. It needs to evaluate its accessibility to parents, its openness to the community, its resilience and responsiveness as an organization, its capacity for change.

When we broach these big issues it becomes apparent just how limited it is to judge a school solely on the examination performance of its pupils at a given time. To do so only shines a narrow beam on school quality and tells us little about causes and consequences. It cannot inform teachers on what to do next; nor does it show us how differently we might view things if we shone a wider beam or pointed it in another direction.

When should evaluation take place?

We have often tended to see assessment and evaluation in similar ways, as activities undertaken at the end of a sequence. Exams are final tests of what has been learned. Evaluations are now a commonplace feature of conferences, workshops: end-of-lesson, end-of-term, end-of-year events. However, like assessment, evaluation may also *precede* events – providing a starting point or baseline. Like assessment it may also be intermittent, ongoing or continuous, formative as well as summative. 'When?', therefore, seems to be a relevant question.

External evaluation, or inspection, can occur at any time in a school's annual cycle. It can be spontaneous, ongoing and unannounced, working on the premise that as the life of school is continuous and dynamic its moods and seasons can be captured at any time. Nonetheless, inspections rarely come at the 'right time', which is when the school is at its consistent best – a state of being it can, in fact, rarely if ever achieve.

The issue of how often inspection should occur has never been satisfactorily resolved. OFSTED used to inspect schools on a four-yearly cycle but have recently moved away from that to a more differentiated and discriminating approach, applying a lighter, or heavier, touch depending on the school's performance. Scottish HMI also adopt a differentiated approach but at the same time offer a guarantee to parents that their child's school will be inspected once in their primary and secondary school life.

In the Netherlands this principle is enshrined in a new law of proportionality which states that inspection (or 'supervision' as it is now renamed) should be in proportion to the quality of a school's self-evaluation: 'this principle expresses respect for the autonomy of the stimulation and support' (Van Amelsvoort, 2001).

Whenever and how often a visit takes place , and whether it takes the form of inspection, quality assurance, hallmarking or Investors in People validation, external evaluation does comprise an event. So when it comes to internal evaluation it is perhaps unsurprising that it should also be seen as an event, an audit once every two or three years. Ferguson and Earley (2001) writing about 'self-inspection' tend to see it in these terms, advocating the use of the OFSTED framework by the school itself with an annual schedule.

However, internal evaluation may be viewed in another way, as built in, and ongoing, an integral part of the day-to-day life of the school and classroom. Just as assessment can be as continuous and seamless as learning itself, so evaluation can be a habit, a reflex, a learned response on the part of pupils and teachers. This does, however, presuppose that pupils and teachers have evaluation tools at their disposal, are comfortable with their use and, like the athlete in training (who relies totally and absolutely on performance feedback), believe such tools to bring tangible benefits in enhancing performance.

This does not preclude the collation of data at a given point, especially in preparation for an external visit, but it then takes the form of collation of existing data rather than the laborious process of creating data and data-gathering instruments. If we ever move wholeheartedly to unannounced inspection it will be in recognition of the maturity of school self-evaluation, able to provide evidence at any given time of the school's state of organisational and psychological health.

Who is it for?

If we were to enter any school in the British Isles and ask 'Who is this evaluation for?' we would get many different answers depending on to whom we put the question. It may be in the interest of national government or the local authority to assure itself of standards, to be able to reply with confidence to parliamentary or council chamber questions. It may be seen as providing information for parents on school choice or as a form of accountability to them for the trust they have invested in the school. Or its primary purpose may be as diagnostic information for the school's internal stakeholders, for teachers or for pupils. It may, on the other hand, be seen as formative data in order to inform development planning. In other words the audience for evaluating is intimately related to purpose.

How we see the main audience for evaluation tells the values-and-purpose story. For this very reason it may be difficult to prioritise its various functions. Evaluation may be viewed as serving multiple

Using the grid below, rank in order of importance from 1 to 6 what you see as the most and least important audiences for self-evaluation. This may be undertaken as an individual or a group activity.

Audience	Rank in order of importance from 1 to 6
for parents	
for the authority	
for school inspectors	
for pupils	
for teachers	
for the local community	

Figure 1.3 Ranking audiences by importance

audiences and diverse purposes. Evaluating teaching and learning may serve teachers' own developmental needs but also provide useful data for appraisal or for the benefit of visiting inspectors. Alternatively, schools may gather data to meet an inspection and, in the process, find it useful for improving classroom practice.

How?

How to evaluate is a subject that can arouse strong passions among researchers and adherents of different schools of thought. There are some for whom evaluation is so precious that it cannot be entrusted to teachers or non-experts. There are those for whom validity and reliability are such sacred canons that virtually nothing reaches their criteria of excellence. There are those who trust only to rigorous objective procedures and others who believe that deeper truths are only accessible through sub-jective methods. There are behaviourists and constructivists, passionate advocates of quantitative as against qualitative techniques, phenom-enologists and positivists, ethnographers and multi-level modellers, advocates of the large-scale and individual case study, proponents of the interview, questionnaire, focus group, observation or myriad other forms of research and evaluation. Advocacy of these, often exclusive, gospels is frequently accompanied by dogma and arcane language which mystify and intimidate teachers. It can serve to exclude them from dialogue and to deskill, conveying the message that this is territory only for the expert and initiated – that teaching is for teachers and evaluation strictly for the evaluators. The arrogance of this position is blind to the fact that teachers are natural evaluators, do it more often and more routinely than those in many other professions, and do it with an eclectic range of tools and strategies.

Synthesis is the key

Synthesis is the key to effective evaluation, says Ernest House (1973). From all the information available, from multiple values and criteria, from multiple methods and multiple stakeholders we arrive at 'an all-things-considered synthesis'. Synthesis is not, however, synonymous with 'definitive' judgement. It is the best, most honest, most considered judgement we can arrive at in the circumstances. All knowledge is conjectural, argued the philosopher Karl Popper, and we know from our own experience that even the most definitive of scientific truths is likely to be contradicted a few years down the line.

Thinking about schools, the 'How good?' will always be open to new insights, new interpretations and new knowledge about organisations and the mysterious unfathomable beings who inhabit them. 'How good is our school?' will also be answered from different individual standpoints, from different status positions, with differing vested interest, motive and motivation.

Chelimsky and Shadish (1999) suggest three perspectives on evaluation which they call the accountability perspective, the knowledge perspective and the developmental perspective. Drawing on this we may compare purposes, audience, users, and the interrelationship of internal and external evaluation

These provide a useful framework for re-examining the question 'What's in it for schools?' Being clear about purpose, audience and providers will put self-evaluation on firmer ground and make the school better prepared and better able to respond to external evaluation, whatever form it takes.

	Accountability perspective	*Knowledge perspective*	*Developmental perspective*
Purpose	To provide data on performance, effectiveness and value for money	To generate new insights about quality of what matters – e.g. leadership, ethos, learning and teaching	To strengthen the capacity of the school for self-improvement
Audience	Public and parents	School management and teachers	Teachers, pupils, parents, leadership
Provider(s)	School management	Teachers, pupils, school management	Teachers, pupils, parents, support staff, school management
Internal/ external relationship	Summative External evaluation supported by data from self-evaluation	Diagnostic Primarily through self-evaluation	Formative Primarily self-evaluation with external critical friend' support

Figure 1.4 Three perspectives on evaluation

2 Internal and external evaluation – two sides of a coin

'Truths are the product of evidence, argument and construction rather than of authority' – Jerome Bruner, 1966

We have argued in chapter 1 that evaluation has to become an integral part of our work. Whether we are teachers, headteachers, inspectors, policy makers or professors of education we benefit from the knowledge of how well we are performing and the extent to which our own judgement agrees with the judgements that others bring to our work. In this respect we have made real progress in the last decade. The once secret garden, closed to all but a select few jealously guarding the territory, is now open to scrutiny at both school and national levels. More and more we have come to realise that making things better for young people demands a commitment to evaluating what we are offering on a monthly, weekly, and daily basis. Evaluation is becoming a habit rather than an ad hoc, one-off response to a crisis or unexpected review.

Internal and external evaluation

The distinction between 'internal' and 'external' evaluation may seem obvious, but it is worth teasing out nonetheless. In this book we are using the term 'internal evaluation' to mean the monitoring of any aspect of a school's work by its key stakeholders: its staff, its pupils, its parents. The term 'stakeholder' is an important one because it describes those who have a direct stake in the welfare and performance of the school. Their judgements stem from self-interest. They are not objective observers nor do they bring a neutral, disinterested perspective to the interpretation of data. For the most part they care about how good their schools are.

Internal evaluation is usually seen as synonymous with 'self-' evaluation. This term is used not just in the individual sense but in a corporate, or communal, sense. It is about a collective gathering of data. It involves teachers and school leaders coming to judgements based on their first-hand knowledge of what is happening in classrooms, workshops and laboratories throughout the school. It requires that pupils have in their possession the tools to reflect on their learning. It means parents rendering their judgement of the school's performance and accountability, particularly in relation to their own children. Self-evaluation takes place whenever teachers consider more effective layouts for their classroom, when a school considers the need to change a reading scheme or seeks to improve the style and tone of its letters and reports to parents. Whenever existing provision is examined with a view to its improvement internal evaluation is at work, often informally but increasingly in a self-conscious and systematic way.

External evaluation is used to mean the review and reporting on a school's work by people who are not part of the school's organisation. External evaluators may belong to different agencies and come with different mandates. Local authority personnel, inspectors and advisers, have long played a role in reviewing school performance, with varying combinations of audit and support, feedback and advice. As employers (or quasi-employers), authority personnel occupy a more ambivalent position than national inspectorates. Indeed the more they themselves are evaluated in terms of how their schools perform, the more ambivalent their position as 'external' evaluators becomes.

In recognition of this it is increasingly common for authorities to commission evaluations from outside bodies: research agencies, universities or consultancy companies. The burgeoning bidding economy with its proliferating new funding sources – the Challenge Fund, the Excellence Fund, the New Opportunities Fund, the Single Regeneration Budget – all build in requirements for evaluation, so providing a new income stream for external agencies. Alongside these are agencies which offer a prestigious hallmark, attesting to the quality of the organisation on the basis of external review or 'inspection'. These include Investors in People (IIP), the European Foundation for Quality Management (EQFM), ISO 9000.

Alternative forms of external evaluation include coalitions of schools evaluating one another. The Latin American Heads Conference conducts reviews of its own schools by its own members. In Rhode Island, teachers constitute the review body which conducts evaluations of schools within its network. The form of external evaluation which most closely touches the life of schools in the United Kingdom is the programme of inspections regularly carried out by HM Inspectors of Schools: OFSTED in England, HMI in Scotland, Wales and inspectors in Northern Ireland. All of these inspectorates continue to pride themselves on their independence and impartiality of judgement. They aim to provide an independent check of the school's performance in relation to key aspects of the school's priorities and performance. In the four UK inspectorates the criteria on which schools are judged are common, laid down and non-negotiable. OFSTED's recent adoption of school self-evaluation resulted in schools being given the criteria used by inspectors and trained in their use through a series of local authority seminars.

An alternative model of internal/external evaluation is for the external evaluation not to focus on a set of predetermined criteria, or indicators, but to examine the school's own success criteria and evaluate the school in terms of how well it is meeting its own objectives. While such an approach is common to many forms of external evaluation it is less common among inspectorates, although there are situations and contexts, in special or alternative schools, for example, where HMI may find this most appropriate. Its most celebrated case was in the inspection of Summerhill School, where the school's success indicators and those applying to mainstream schools were highly contested by the school itself. It terminated in a case heard at the Royal Courts of Justice in September 2000 at which the school's position was largely vindicated.

Both are needed

An effective system of school evaluation needs to contain elements of both internal and external evaluation. Launching the HM Inspectors of Schools' Audit Unit at a national conference in 1992, its new Director (and one of the authors of this book) used the image of concentric circles (Figure 2.1) to illustrate the all-embracing nature of evaluation in education. The school is placed at the centre, emphasising that it is the prime mover and that, as such, it must concern itself with the questions

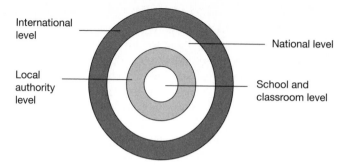

Figure 2.1 Four levels of evaluation

'How good are we?' and 'How do we know?' These questions are addressed to a number of groups but in the first instance to teachers, recognising that it is teachers who make the difference. Their evaluation of their own performance can then be commented on by others – by colleagues, by school leaders, by pupils.

By the same token school leaders evaluate themselves and are also evaluated by others –whether from 'above' – authorities, inspectors, teams of peers, or from 'below' – by teachers, pupils or parents. All of these different facets are encompassed within the notion of 'self evaluation', so it not a simple process of self-justification (as the term might seem to imply) but rather an inbuilt challenge from a multiplicity of perspectives.

Thus the self-evaluating school comes to a judgement of its performance by drawing together these various perspectives and complementing them with pupil performance data. But good schools always want to do better and to know how they compare with other schools, perhaps in the same locality or local authority. So, the second circle provides an external layer of evaluation. With the use of indicators and benchmarks, the local authority can carry out its own evaluation of its schools. At the same time it may itself be engaged in evaluation, considering the extent to which the performance of its schools is a direct reflection of how well it is supporting and challenging them. In concert with 'How good are our schools?' it also poses the question 'How good are we as an authority?'

The third circle represents the national level, an external evaluation at a further remove from the school and authority. In posing the question

'How good are our schools?' it is concerned with the deeper question of 'How good is the system we provide to sustain and improve the quality of our country's education?' To answer the question the Ministry of Education may commission an independent body to carry out an evaluation (for example, the commissioning of System 3's evaluation of the Inspectorate in Scotland); it may draw on inspectorate evidence of quality and standards; it may look to its schools and authorities to evaluate its effectiveness.

The key question in the fourth circle is 'How do we compare with other countries?' This brings into the picture external sources of evaluation of international agencies such as the Organisation for Economic Cooperation and Development (OECD), UNESCO, the Third International Mathematics and Science Study (TIMSS) and the European Commission. All of these have, in different ways, used international data to compare relative quality and standards country by country, for example in relation to student attainment, costs and resourcing, literacy and numeracy, staying-on rates, or costs. In 2000 the European Commission commissioned its own set of sixteen key indicators which included the relationship between internal and external evaluation in each of the participating countries. All these international projects have been directed towards shaping national agendas and priorities.

In sum, the message is that self-evaluation is for teachers, schools, local authorities and ministries of education and that the best system combines elements of internal and external evaluation. While in the best of possible worlds they are complementary, they are often in tension, each with their own advocates, making the case for one or the other.

QUESTION:

How would you make the case for internal evaluation:
to teachers?
to parents?
to pupils?
to governors, school boards?

The case for internal evaluation

The case for internal evaluation is made on the grounds of ownership, on the logic that those who are closest to everyday practice are also those best placed to evaluate and improve it. So, in the concentric model, at the core is the school itself with its own inner concentric circles of classrooms, individual teachers and individual pupils. The starting point lies with the Socratic notion of knowing thyself: 'How good am I as a learner, a teacher, a principal teacher or headteacher? The approach rests on a view of educators as self-aware, self-critical, thinking professionals and applies those same criteria to those they attempt to educate. Its primary aim is to establish a climate, or culture, in which there is a shared belief that everyone can make a difference and that school improvement is the right and responsibility of every single member of the educational community. The cornerstone is the belief that making a difference is both invited and achievable.

The greater the sense of belonging the more likely the chance of success. The more the feeling that evaluation is a shared school-wide enterprise the greater the likelihood of people 'owning', or 'stewarding' their investment. The questions raised and discussed in chapter 1 are ones to which staff need answers, and it is important to create the time and space to explore these openly and without prejudice.

- What is the purpose?
- Who is it for?
- Who will carry it out?
- Who will be consulted?
- How much time and energy will it consume?
- How will be results be shown?

An open and critical discourse around these questions lends strength and credibility to the process. Those who engage in self-evaluation are informed insiders with a close and detailed knowledge of the inner workings of their school. Staff come through its doors every day and are immersed in its culture, sometimes at an intuitive level of awareness, sometimes without having had the opportunity or tools to make their implicit understandings into explicit theories. The same applies to pupils, often with a deep and unarticulated level of awareness which has never been afforded the opportunity to become studied and systematic. Parents and governors have less access to that grounded day-to-day knowledge and are, as a consequence, in greater need of opportunities to examine their subjective judgements of quality and standards.

Internal evaluation need not disrupt normal patterns of working. It can be an integral part of school life, embracing key aspects of a school's work, focusing on what matters most to teachers, pupils and parents. As it is undertaken by those who know most about what is going on in classrooms, in departments, in the school overall it needs to be well informed, in the most rigorous sense of that term. That is, data should be scrupulously fair and relevant to the task in hand since the information generated is immediately available to those who are expected to act on it, and because it furnishes an agenda for improvement planning.

QUESTION:

How would you make the case for external evaluation by inspection (OFSTED/HMI):
to teachers?
to parents?
to pupils?
to governors, school boards?

The case for inspection

The case for inspection rests on the need for an external reality check. It may be argued that when self-evaluation is focused, relevant and robust it then removes the need for external verification. However, few if any schools can boast of having fully met those criteria and, ironically, it is usually the most successful of self-evaluators who welcome the external perspective. They welcome it perhaps because they wish to celebrate their efforts, perhaps for affirmation that they have got it right, perhaps because they welcome a further critical eye. Schools still struggling with self-evaluation may be less welcoming of inspection but need it more. This is true not only of schools but of a wide spectrum of public and private agencies.

The concern to achieve excellence in public accountability has brought a sharply increased focus on the importance of inspection and external quality assurance in all aspects of the public services – all aspects of education; child care; social work services; the police and fire services, the prison service. These have been traditional public concerns. But it is interesting to detect a changing public mood and political commitment which is translating these expectations to other services including the health service, the judicial service and the creation of new inspectorates and quality assurance agencies.

(Osler, 1999)

Inspection systems have their critics, and none more than OFSTED. Few, however, argue for the abolition of inspection. The self-styled watchdog body, the Office For Standards in Education (OFSTIN), said this following its conference in 1996:

No one argued that external inspection had no role in the public education system or in the process of school improvement. The public accountability of schools require quality and control that includes an element of external inspection which is open and transparent.

There are many different models, but all hold in common the view that external monitoring plays an important role in both accountability and improvement. These are some of the principles on which the case for inspection rests:

- The government is committed to rigorous inspection as a key part of its drive to raise standards in our schools.
- To be widely respected, an inspectorate needs to be noted for its independence, rigour and fairness.
- Inspections should take place against a framework of agreed criteria, or indicators, which have been published and made available to schools. These may also serve as the basis for self-evaluation.
- The primary focus should be on the quality of learning and teaching and the conditions which support that.

- Inspections should be thorough and evidence-based.
- Inspections should recognise and affirm good practice as well as identifying areas for improvement.
- Fairness must be a pre-eminent concern. Draft inspection reports should be discussed before publication with the headteacher, education authority and chair of governors or school board with attention to accuracy and additional (or contrary) evidence.
- It must be recognised that inspection is inevitably stressful and steps should be taken to reduce stress as far as is possible.

It is common for inspectors to have been trained to recognise and respond to stress, approaching inspections well aware of the pressures faced by staff. What is less often acknowledged is that it can also be a highly stressful experience for the inspector herself, who will rarely relish giving highly critical feedback and breaking bad news to fellow professionals. Most inspectors have been teachers themselves, and many will have been inspected at some point in their careers. A recent study (Bennett, 2001) of the Scottish Inspectorate found that HMI, having been teachers themselves, was a key factor in how they were received and respected by staff.

Summarising questionnaire data, the author found that there was:

- a strong recognition of the need for inspection;
- general agreement with the findings of the inspection team;
- a positive contribution made by inspection to the development of the school and, where the inspection report was generally positive, the raised morale of the teachers.

But she also noted:

- an unacceptable level of stress;
- a need for more time for class teachers to have discussions with inspectors;
- a need for more specific recommendations where criticisms were offered;
- a concern that inspectors did not have sufficient knowledge of the school context;
- the criticism that the Inspectors based their judgements on a limited sample of a school's work.

The Education and Training Inspectorate in Northern Ireland recorded similar findings based on written evaluations provided voluntarily by the principals of schools and colleges at the end of inspections. The report (2000) '*Education & Training Inspectorate Evaluation of Inspection 1996–8*' stated that:

> Written comments indicated that the inspection afforded staff the opportunity to discuss their work with other professionals and most appreciated the evaluations, and found the advice they received helpful. Many principals commented on the positive benefits gained from inspection. A small number, however, considered that the inspection produced unhelpful effects and lowered the morale of staff.

The pleasures of the secret garden

When one of the co-authors undertook his first inspection some twenty-five years ago, procedures were fairly informal and ad hoc. The atmosphere was cosy, the findings were exclusive to the inner club of educationalists in their own 'secret garden'. The timetable was leisurely, and there were little or no agreed criteria on which to base individual evaluations. The whole process seemed to focus on the professional players while parents and pupils were mostly unaware of what was going on. The reports were for the Secretary of State for Scotland but few, if any, found their way into the 'red box'. This is not to say that some hard-hitting inspection and reporting did not take place, but they went largely unnoticed by the world outside education and were often judged to be unfair by headteachers and teachers who were kept in the dark about the factors on which the evaluations were based. So there was a mystique about the whole inspection process which some took a delight in perpetuating.

Inspection today is different. The most progressive inspectorates operate to an agreed and published code of practice whose aim is to ensure that inspections are independent, responsive, fair and open. Procedures are made available to schools, parents, governing bodies and school boards. Increasingly all aspects of the process, including reports, are available on the Internet. Great care is taken to ensure that all parties to an inspection are aware of the procedures and the timetable. In Scotland, for example, the head receives a letter with detailed briefing notes, written in plain English, for staff, parents, school boards and pupils. Every parent receives a letter explaining the purposes of the inspection, its scope and range, what happens in the process, and how HMI reach their conclusions. It puts the question 'How are you involved as a parent?' and explains how their children will be involved, talks about the contribution of the lay member of the inspection team, describes the reporting format and sets out what happens after an inspection.

Twin dangers

Critics of internal evaluation point out that it can be self-deluding while critics of external inspection argue that it leads to a culture of dependency. Both are valid concerns. Knowing yourself is not a simple and unproblematic concept. Indeed, individuals and organisations can invest considerable energies in deluding themselves. 'When ignorance is bliss it is folly to be wise' was the theme tune of a 1940s radio programme, a reminder that people and organisations alike do not always relish their frailties being exposed, even to themselves. The more open and penetrating the self-evaluation the greater the degree of anxiety. Recognising the sensitivity of the enterprise and alleviating anxiety is, therefore, the first step in evaluation whether internal or external. The second step is having a shared and open agenda for school improvement, an agreed development plan with priorities for action and measures to evaluate success, along with open reporting to mirror and complement external reporting. The school needs, above all else, to base any strategy for improvement on rigorous and planned monitoring of what actually happens in the classroom, in the laboratory and in the workshop.

When ownership of evaluation is seen to lie outside the school, inspection is seen as something which is 'done to you' and inspection as belonging to inspectors. The subterfuge that takes place prior to an inspection betrays a lack of ownership. The Standing International Conference of Central and General Inspectorates of Education (SICI) found, on the basis of their analysis of European systems:

> A great deal of research into educational innovation has demonstrated that control which is too intrusive does not lead to real improvement in quality but rather to an equivalent of 'teaching-to-the-test' namely a 'teaching-to-the regulations'.

While a standard and publicly available framework is essential to meet the need for consistent and fair reporting, schools and parents may be more interested in an agenda which meets their needs. It is a pertinent criticism that no matter how good the inspectors are, they are not 'insiders' who teach week in and week out. They walk in and they can walk away, sometimes leaving a high level of stress in their wake. A further note of caution is offered by Scotland's Senior Chief Inspector.

> Despite the importance of external objective evaluation, we also have to avoid the danger of what I might call inspection dependency, that is, the assumption that continuous improvement can only be brought about by the 'threat' of inspection. There has to be a strong will to effect improvement on the basis of professional self-evaluation. There are clear dangers of self-evaluation becoming confused with self-delusion, but with a shared and open agenda for improvement, and the moderation of self-evaluation by external commentary, this can be avoided. (Osler, 1999)

The Scottish guidelines 'How Good is Our School?', were designed to help schools avoid these twin dangers and to take an increased share in the ownership of inspection. The current OFSTED model has drawn on the Scottish approach, evolving rapidly under the Labour government from a position where self-evaluation was overtly rejected by the Chief Inspector to a position in which self-evaluation is seen as lying right at the heart of the process. OFSTED now argues that to be maximally effective evaluation by the school 'should draw from the criteria and indicators used in inspection, and should employ similar techniques'. Thus while serving different purposes, self-evaluation and external evaluation reinforce the commitment of all of the key players, in and out of the school, to evaluate what they are doing.

SICI, mentioned above, are currently exploring an approach to external evaluation which would centre on the school's capacity to evaluate itself. In other words, it suggests that inspection might start with the question 'How good is self-evaluation in your school?' A document produced for the Bertelsmann Foundation (MacBeath, 2000) proposed the following eight categories:

1. Clarity of purposes
2. Transparency of criteria
3. Sharing of commitment
4. Availability of tools
5. Accessibility of data
6. Rigour of application
7. Dissemination of findings
8. Effectiveness of impact

Each category is accompanied by a series of questions and examples as illustrated in Figure 2.2.

The purposes of self-evaluation have been thought through critically and articulated in school documentation and dialogue. There is clarity about its various purposes (audit or summative assessment, diagnostic, formative, or for accountability) and appropriateness of these for different tasks and audiences.

QUESTIONS
Have purposes been widely discussed within the school?
Are purposes expressed in plain jargon-free language?
Are different purposes understood by teachers?
What efforts have been made to communicate purposes to wider audiences? For example, pupils? parents?

EXAMPLES
- documentary evidence of purpose and rationale in school handbooks, development plans or evaluation schedules
- examples from teachers of different kinds of evaluations illustrating inherent purposes
- group discussions with pupils to ascertain their understanding of self-evaluation
- parental surveys to identify people's understanding of why self-evaluation is important

Figure 2.2 1. Clarity of purposes

Accountability

Public reporting of school performance is underpinned by a belief in accountability, the overriding purpose served by school inspections. While the press for accountability may be seen as intrusive and controlling, few disagree that it has its place. The term does, however, assume different meanings and takes different forms from one country to the next. In the Netherlands (McGlynn, 2000) accountability is described in these terms: 'Accountability is the principle that all in education, who have a responsibility for the provision of good education, give a public account about their targets, their actual achievement and performance and their plans for improvement'.

The Hungarians say this: 'Accountability in education starts from a focus on the needs and expectations of its stakeholders', while Norway reminds us that a definition of accountability needs to emphasise the question: 'for whom are we here?'

Linda Darling-Hammond (1995) suggests five types of educational accountability which, adapted to a UK context, may be expressed as three key ideas: the legal/statutory, the professional/moral, and the political/market.

Legal/statutory accountability relates to the statutory duties of national governments, states, local authorities and schools to provide an appropriate range of educational services, to provide best value for money, to set national standards and goals and to be accountable for using tax payers' money.

Professional/moral accountability means that 'all professionals engaged in education are accountable to their students for the quality of education they deliver, or manage, or inspect'. This is a recognition that education has as one of its prime aims the development of young people's knowledge, understanding, skills, confidence and social values. Thus the idea of moral accountability needs to be placed alongside the professional.

Political/market accountability refers to a government conception of the market, to consumers and stakeholders who need to be kept informed of how public services are being delivered and whether they represent value for money.

The *common ground*:

*   Accountability is about taking account of the views, aspirations and expectations of the stakeholders in informing and shaping policy and procedures.
*   Accountability is about the providers informing stakeholders of the data that matter and which can be gauged against goals and targets.
*   Accountability is about using the data to inform a public and ongoing debate about quality in schools, school systems and the country as a whole – with the aim of improving educational provision.

Tensions

There can, however, be tensions between the right of a school to self-evaluate with its own improvement targets and the school system which sets overall targets. These may be more or less demanding and perhaps out of step with those set by the school or the local authority. Striking the balance between freedom of action at school or local level and conformity to national or state guidelines is a central issue in almost all countries. For example, in New Zealand, ten years on from the advent of 'Tomorrow's Schools', concern has been expressed that 'in some cases the reforms have been seen as required only to satisfy demands of external accountability and as a compliance burden on schools' (McGlynn, 2000).

It is not only in New Zealand that such concerns are voiced. It is a current theme in the United States and Canada and, closer to home, Scotland and England have been accused of a culture of compliance (McBride, 2001, Mitchell, 2001). It is charged that targets have been imposed arbitrarily and inappropriately and have undermined rather than enhanced the improvement efforts of schools.

The lesson, at ministerial, authority, school and classroom level, is to ensure that, as far as possible, the 'twin towers' of internal and external evaluation are mutually supportive. In short, everyone seeking to promote excellence in education should:

*   recognise that the agenda for the public service of education should derive from the interests of its 'clients' rather than the sometimes vested interests of the producers;

- articulate clearly what they are setting out to do, in terms that their stakeholders can understand;
- regularly monitor and evaluate their own work, against indicators that are understood and agreed by those required to use them;
- provide well-organised and robust information for external monitoring and evaluation;
- exemplify practice which is clearly related to information collected;
- be open to public scrutiny.

Applying these criteria to inspection regimes in different countries would give us some distinctively different answers. In England, the approach to 'failing schools' and to 'naming and shaming' has been criticised for its adverse effects on teacher morale, retention and recruitment (see, for example, James Learmonth's volume in this series, Cedric Cullingford's *When Inspectors Call* and Michael Fielding's recent critique of Labour's first term of office, *Four Years' Hard Labour*). In Scotland, for example, there are also schools in difficulty and they are also the subject of published reports, but care has been taken by HMI to avoid the overt stigma that is carried by 'special measures' in England. Writing in the *Education Review* (Spring 2001), Hilary Bill, primary school headteacher, arguing for a change in language and labelling says:

> An OFSTED inspection and its reporting procedures still carry the threat of public humiliation. Our school was named and shamed on the front page of *The Times* in 1997, quite unjustifiably as it turned out ... The school was removed from special measures in November 1997 but we did not make the front page of *The Times* on that occasion.
>
> (p.67)

A range of alternative propositions have been put forward to make inspection more friendly, evidence-based, fair, cost-effective or valid. These are some ideas contained in a special issue of *Education Review* (Spring 2001) entitled *Inspection and Accountability*:

- provide proactive support for schools in difficulty rather than wait for an inspection to announce it;
- include teachers as integral members of inspection teams (perhaps as a majority);

- license schools as self-evaluating, the licence being renewable every five years or so;
- shorten lead time before an inspection as close to the event as possible (a week?);
- mandate a period of time (1–2 days) for the inspection team to spend in the community before visiting the school.

Reciprocity

Perhaps the single most contested issue in external and internal evaluation is that of reciprocity. 'How reciprocal is the relationship between internal and external evaluation?' The Dutch academic Frans Leeuw (2001) suggests two key dimensions of reciprocity which he calls the 'give and take' and the 'you too–me too' dimensions. The first of these refers to the balance between what is given *to* external evaluators and what they give back to the school. The second dimension refers to the transparency of 'evaluability' on both sides. So, for example, is the inspection team as open as they ask the school to be? Are they equally prepared to be evaluated and reported on publicly?

Leeuw goes on to suggest nine 'assumptions' that flow from reciprocity:

- That when evaluators, or inspectors, take reciprocity into account the level of trust between evaluators and evaluands (those being evaluated) will increase.
- That the more the relationship is characterised by trust, the more the evaluators will take into account things that really matter to the evaluands.
- That the more the relationship rests on trust the more the evaluands will act upon the findings. Trust acts as the incentive to listen and therefore to be more predisposed to act.
- That when reciprocity is observed the greater the probability that relevant and acceptable norms and standards will be used.
- That the more reciprocal the relationship the longer the period that evaluands will remain positive about the contribution of the external body with raised motivation to continue the relationship.
- That when reciprocity is taken seriously the less the likelihood of 'pillarisation', the tendency for people to argue their particular corner: their department, their class, their subject.

- That the more the evaluating body opens itself to scrutiny and critique the more the evaluands will give credibility to the office and be willing to act on its advice.
- That where reciprocity is observed the evaluators will place more and more credence on the self-evaluation of the school and reduce costs of external inspection.
- That with greater reciprocity data will be richer. There will less likelihood of cheating and, in summary, a more comprehensive view of school quality and standards.

QUESTIONS:

Could these nine assumptions be turned into a set of indicators which might be used at the next OFSTED or HMI inspection?
Which of these are you most and least comfortable with?

These may be called 'assumptions' because they rest on an act of faith. They rest on a belief that when these conditions are observed evaluation will be fairer, more democratic and more effective and will get closer to the truth. However, not all will necessarily hold and some principles may be more fundamental and valid than others. All will depend on two invisible dimensions: power and high stakes.

We have to consider whether there is an equal measure of power on both sides and if not where the power lies within the relationship. However great the trust and reciprocity between a school and an OFSTED inspection team if it comes to a stand-off there is no doubt as to where the power lies. Related to this is the high-stakes nature of the event. A highly critical report may not have severe consequences for the inspecting team, but it will for the school deemed to have serious weaknesses or put into special measures.

This will be true of almost any inspection system because its members bring with them a mandate and an authority which it would be duplicitous to hide. Part of building the trust, therefore, requires inspectors to be clear and upfront about the parameters of reciprocity and who has the final word. Within this framework an inspection may be congenial, rigorous and challenging. That should always be the defining characteristic of the process.

3 Evaluating teaching

'We must learn to know what we see rather than seeing what we already know'
– Abraham Heschel

More than at any other period in our lifetime the quality of teaching has assumed a high public profile and become a contested political issue. In this climate the burden falls more heavily on external inspection to monitor standards and to report to ministers, parents and public on the performance of teachers. The introduction of performance management and the debate (mainly heated) over performance-related pay have further raised the stakes. At the same time new and far-reaching responsibilities have been given to schools themselves to make judgements of quality, not simply of teaching but of teachers.

Evaluating the quality of teachers and teaching is not new. It has, since schools were first invented, been a preoccupying topic of conversation among pupils, relayed with enthusiasm to parents and transmitted within informal neighbourhood networks. Headteachers have for decades had their own informal league tables of teacher quality whether through first-hand knowledge or the institutional intelligence that seems to seep through classroom walls and escape from the rumour mills. Better to have more formal, open and honest systems of appraisal. Or so it is argued.

In a climate where the stakes are high it is crucial to be clear about the terminology we use and the assumptions we bring to the evaluation process. We now commonly speak of teaching and learning as if they were one word – teaching and learning – carrying within it a suggestion of an inseparable connection. Since teaching is always directed to learning it is easy to assume the corollary: that learning is a necessary product of teaching. Indeed the confusion has often been compounded by evaluation – both inspection and self-evaluation – which has tended to focus on teaching, or even the characteristics of the teacher themself, as proxy measures for the quality of pupil learning.

Teacher effectiveness is a fruitful field of inquiry because so much of teacher behaviour is overt and recordable and covers a wide repertoire of activity. What teachers do can make for interesting theatre with the classroom as the stage in which the teacher is the main player and the one through whom the drama unfolds. Observations of what learners are learning is a much less developed field of inquiry. While pupil behaviour is also open to recording and analysis, pupils tend to play a more supporting and passive role in the classroom and their overt behaviour may yield few clues as to what or how they are thinking. The jokey characterisation of classrooms as places where thirty children watch an adult at work is not too remote from the truth.

There are two possible starting points for evaluating teaching and learning. We can start with the teaching and work back to the learner, or start with the learner and work in the other direction. Both have their own validity but will yield two quite different kinds of insights. The next chapter takes learning as its point of departure. This chapter takes teaching as its starting point.

From teaching to learning

The teaching-to-learning approach is expressed cogently in the OFSTED guidelines for inspection:

> Evaluation of the quality and impact of teaching is central to inspection. . . . The effectiveness of teaching and the consequent rate, breadth, depth and consolidation of pupils' learning are intrinsically connected. It is the skill of rigorous and perceptive inspection to find, illustrate and evaluate the links between the two.
>
> (*OFSTED Handbook* 2000, p.45)

It is implicit in any observation of teaching that it is a means to an end and not an end in itself. However, classroom observation does not always pursue these connections. As teachers our first experience of being evaluated was the 'crit', a shorthand description for its perceived purpose. It was conducted by a tutor from the college of education or university. This individual sat at the back or the room for a half an hour to an hour, sometimes conducting a short, and not always successful, postscript to the lesson, a demonstration of how it ought to be done. His or her evaluation of your teaching was written some time later in the green book below your lesson notes as in this (real) example:

> A lively and interesting presentation which helped the class to settle down well. Knowledge and use of names helped to keep discipline and respond to children who had their hands up. The peripatetic movement up and down the rows made it less easy to scan what was going on: a better position at the front of the class would help. Blackboard skills still need a bit of work as does pacing of the lesson. Being 'caught short' by the bell left an untidy end to what was overall an excellent lesson.

The subjective nature of these 'crits' was to be the brunt of some criticism, as was the somewhat unfocused and generalised set of comments. This led to a more systematic approach being developed, equipping tutors with a more comprehensive list of competencies covering the gamut of a lesson from entry, presentation, control, questioning, pace, variety, summarising and so on. These were to prove no less contentious or popular than the more open-ended 'crit', and the pendulum has swung more or less continuously between making competencies more detailed and specific on the one hand and more general and open-ended on the other.

Direct observation has a lot to commend it, and a great deal can be 'picked up' by an astute observer, able to 'read' the situation in all its interlocking parts and internal dynamic, bringing to it what Elliot Eisner (1991) calls the 'enlightened eye'. He writes:

> The ability to see what counts is one of the features that differentiates novices from experts. According it to Berliner (1988), novice teachers tend to describe virtually everything they can in the classroom when they are asked to state what is going on there. The expert knows what to neglect. Knowing what to neglect means having a sense for

the significant and possessing a framework that makes the search for the significant efficient.

(p. 34)

Such skills have, for many years, been the stock-in-trade of school inspectors. However, reliance on the individual skills and personal enlightenment of the observer casts doubt on the overall reliability of the method. Experiments on inter-rate reliability have revealed discrepancies among observers evaluating the same situation, sometimes relatively small but significant enough to cross over, or fall short of, the critical threshold between pass and fail, or between good and excellent. The difference between Olympic judges' scores of 5.5 and 5.9, while on the statistical surface extremely close, does in effect describe the difference between 'excellent' and 'poor'.

The need to find more objective approaches has led to a proliferation of rating scales and observation schedules, enabling teacher behaviours to be quantified and indices devised to reveal, for example, the proportion of class time spent on teacher talk or pupil talk, on whole-class teaching, group work, individual work, the proportion of the time taken up with disciplinary issues, with administrative tasks or simple time-wasting.

Over time observation techniques categories have become more sophisticated and probing, including questions such as:

- How much talk is pupil-initiated or teacher-initiated?
- What is the nature of the talk? – Information-giving? Hypothesising? Evaluating?
- How is talk distributed? Who gets attention and who doesn't?
- What part does gender, or 'ability' or ethnic status play in the trans-action?

The further and deeper these questions go, however, the more qualitative and interpretative they become, relying more and more on observer skills and less on less on the instrument itself. The more probing the questions become the more they highlight the tensions between the objective and subjective: teaching as art, teaching as science.

It is a tension that is unlikely to be easily resolved. Those in the scientific/objectification camp continue to try and perfect schedules which will finally eliminate observer bias. Those leaning towards the subjective/intuitive camp, on the other hand, argue for connoisseur-ship: cultivating the enlightened eye that is able to 'see' the subliminal chemistry and dynamics of the classroom. While the 'objectifiers' have demonstrated just how much could be learned from statistical profiles – percentage of time on and off task, balance of time given to teaching v. control, preponderance of providing as against eliciting information – 'the 'subjectifiers' have found support in the work on emotional intel-ligence and intuition, which demonstrates the acuity of some people to 'read' complex social situations in which events are simultaneous, over-lapping and not easily separable. Eisner says this:

> It is usually not the incidence of an event that gives it significance, but its quality and its relationship to the context in which it functions. Counting the incidence of isolated features may obscure rather than reveal what is important in the setting.

> (p.167)

Quantifying events can complement qualitative observation, as Eisner illustrates with the case of four independent researchers observing a forty-five-minute videotape of exemplary teaching, each coming up with new and different insights as they probed beneath the surface of the lesson. For example, one of the four focused not simply on the distribution of the teacher's questions by gender but the nature of the teacher's follow-up probing with boys and with girls. Examining probing in terms of its neutral or challenging nature and its positive or negative evaluation by the teacher, he found that, while positives and negatives were more or less evenly distributed by gender, follow-up challenges only ever occurred with the boys. Such observations might all too easily slip past the less enlightened eye.

A further probing set of questions is provided by Michael Fielding (2000), evaluating the subtext of classroom interaction. He suggests nine categories, each one containing within it a list of simple but probing questions. For example, in the first category, 'Speaking', he poses the following seven questions:

- Who is allowed to speak?
- To whom are they allowed to speak?
- What are they allowed to speak about?

- What language is encouraged/allowed?
- Who decides the answers to these questions?
- How are these decisions made?
- How, when, where, to whom, and how often are those decisions communicated?

An example of what can be seen by perceptive observers is provided by Kounin (1970) in his classic study of teacher behaviour in which he identified a range of subtle, almost subliminal, skills for which he invented a new language (Figure 3.1).

Dimensions of classroom management (Kounin 1970)

'Withitness': An awareness of events going on around even though not directly visible e.g. teacher at blackboard with her back to the class says, 'Get on with your work, Angela.'

Overlapping: when the teacher has two or more things to deal with simultaneously e.g. while engaged in one-to-one tuition also signals disapproval (a 'desist' to a misbehaving group).

Dangles: when a teacher starts an activity then leaves it hanging e.g. teacher starts reading from a book then stops to attend to some behavioural issue.

'Flip-flops': when a teacher starts an activity, then begins another, then returns to the first e.g. teacher says to pupils to put away spelling and get out arithmetic books, then asks pupils about their spelling.

Thrusts: when the teacher interrupts pupil activities, perhaps without sensitivity to the group, or individual's readiness e.g. pupils are working in pairs and the teacher stops their activity to address the whole class.

Overdwelling: when a teacher stays on one issue beyond what was necessary or engaging e.g. teacher goes back repeatedly over the same ground, resulting in some pupils, most, or all becoming bored and disengaged.

Fragmentation: when the teacher slows down the pace of the lesson by breaking her instructions into small units instead of a whole, e.g. the teacher takes five minutes to get pupils to change from one activity to the next by a series of detailed, over-elaborated steps.

Figure 3.1 Kounin's dimensions of classroom management

Much more recently Hay–McBer's (2000) study for the DFEE (available on their website) identifies a range of measurable teacher behaviours but complements these with two other facets of effective teachers: one, professional characteristics such as respect for others, information-seeking, teamworking, flexibility, a passion for learning, and two, classroom climate, which takes as its starting point what the classroom feels like for those on the receiving end.

Pupils' perceptions of 'the good teacher' tend to come to a remarkably consistent set of conclusions. For example, Ted Wragg and his colleagues (2000) concluded from a large survey of pupils in England that, in order of frequency, pupils prioritised:

- Helps when pupils are stuck.
- Explains clearly.
- Can control the class.
- Has a sense of humour.
- Is friendly/has a good relationship with the pupils.
- Interesting and enjoyable lessons.
- Listens to children.

These are very close to those qualities nominated by pupils in the NUT study (MacBeath et al. 1995) by David Frost in Hertfordshire (2001) and in the German example as illustrated in Figure 3.3.

Inspectors – observed and observing

Over the years inspection has been subject to many swings of the pendulum in an attempt to find the point of balance: a form of evaluation that would be acceptable to the observed and would also meet social scientists' demand for validity and reliability.

OFSTED guidelines illustrate a movement towards a fuller, more measured and complex evaluation of teaching. Rather than simply relying on observation of the teacher, the inspector is advised to move between watching what the teacher is doing and what the pupil is doing, focusing in particular on one or two pupils so as to follow a continuous thread of teaching-learning.

Combining structured observation with scrutiny of pupils' work requires considerable interpretive skills in reaching a definitive judgement, grading the teacher on a seven-point scale (with an eight being reserved for inability to reach a judgement). The award of the grade is supported by an explanatory paragraph as illustrated in the following from the OFSTED *Handbook* (p. 44):

Extract from a subject report: teaching of English, *Julius Caesar*

> Pupils learned little in the lesson about the nature of Shakespearean language and its emotional and verbal structure. They made no progress in their understanding because of a line-by-line translation of Mark Antony's speech into modern English by the teacher, whose own knowledge of blank verse and patterns of dramatic rhetoric did not match the demands and complexity of the text. Because the material was never given a dramatic context, pupils' understanding of the speaker and the situation remained at an unsatisfactory level. No demands were made on pupils' imagination and no opportunities for critical and interpretative reading. Behaviour was dutifully acquiescent.
>
> Teaching overall: poor teaching (6)

This excerpt illustrates the complexity of the task, the nature and scope of the inferences drawn and the categorical judgement reached. However fair and valid the critique, evaluations such as these must take into account the limitations of the methodology. However well-prepared and enlightened the classroom observer there will be always be limitations to what can be 'seen'. The observer becomes, at least initially, the most significant person in the room. An inspector can never be a neutral invisible presence, wherever she sits or however small she tries to make herself. She may achieve wallpaper status over time but that is only likely to happen over an extended period. How long it takes to become invisible is primarily dependent on the observer's purpose in being there, the intrusiveness of their presence and, above all, the high-stakes (or perceived high-stakes) nature of their business.

This puts the inspector, more than any other classroom visitor, at a disadvantage. Her classroom visit is always invariably perceived as high stakes. The inspector is never in the classroom long enough to become inconsequential. Her prior negotiations with the teacher and class are minimal or non-existent. Observations are curtailed within the observation framework and their reporting protocol. What the inspector might never discover about the *Julius Caesar* lesson is whether the lesson had been tailored to meet her expectations. It is, after all, not unusual for teachers to do their homework on any given inspector's preferences and predilections. The 'dutiful acquiescence' noted by the inspector may, in fact, say more about the particular occasion than about the real quality of teacher–pupil relationships in that classroom. It is not uncommon for children to think they are 'being good' and helping their teacher out by being passively acquiescent.

From the point of view of the three main sets of players in the classroom we can appreciate the difficulties in getting it right.

The observer is sensitive to her status as a newcomer. She tries to be unobtrusive, to encourage pupils and teachers to be carry on as 'normal'. She is aware of the shortness of the time she has with the class – thirty to forty minutes – and the high-stakes nature of her task. She is aware that the teacher is aware of her presence and that pupils are on their best behaviour. She tries, within the short time available to her, to reach an honest judgement of the quality of the teaching and to have the courage to record that judgement in categorical terms. She recognises that while she relies on her prior experience she is also restricted by 'habits of seeing', that these will frame how she interprets what she sees.

The teacher is acutely conscious of the observer's presence. He has alerted the class beforehand and asked for their co-operation. He knows they will rise to the occasion. Although he tries hard to behave as normal and to teach the class he is aware that despite himself the observer has become the main 'audience' of the lesson. In his sweep of the classroom he looks for reassurance, attempting to interpret the body language of the observer. He is aware of his own distraction and becomes concerned that it will inhibit his normal fluency and informality with the class.

The pupils are aware of the visitor from the moment they enter the room. The have been told beforehand of the importance of the situation. They are not sure of her provenance or authority or really why she is there, but they are aware of the difference in their teacher's behaviour and the general ethos of the classroom, which feels more tense and guarded than usual. If they turn casually sideways they can see the visitor and gauge her reaction to the teacher. They are disappointed at the lack of the usual humour and banter and are unsure of what will be acceptable. Some decide it is safer to take no risks and remain quiet.

Taken together these provide some, but not all, of the contextual factors in which observations take place. We have to remind ourselves that observations have a time and a place and that classrooms have their histories as well as their present. It is a sobering reminder, which we know from our own school days, that much of the 'underlife' of the classroom is beyond even the reach of the teacher who has spent a year or more with her pupils.

The story is told, perhaps apocryphal, of the inspector touring the classroom examining pupils' work . He stops to admire the jottings of one little girl, then draws the class's attention to what she has written. 'Do you mind', he says, 'if I read this out to the rest of the class? It is so beautifully written. Its form and cadences are so well chosen.' He reads:

Yesterday, yesterday, yesterday
Grief, grief, grief
Tomorrow, tomorrow, tomorrow
Relief, relief, relief.

'What a wonderful poem,' he says to the girl. 'Could you share with us how you came to write these lines?' The little girl, looking up at him, replies:

'Please sir, those are my spelling mistakes.'

The story, whatever its origins in fact, does point up the significance of context. Whether the teacher is being evaluated through direct observation of her behaviour, or as reflected in her pupils' work, it does require to be situated in both past and present. If teachers are to be evaluated through the work their pupils produce it can only make sense within the repertoire of that child's overall progress and attitude, and normatively in relation to others in the class, school and community. The extent to which that piece of individual work, in fact, reflects the competence of the teacher may also require a sophisticated judgement.

Observing teaching – from the inside

All of these caveats about observation apply with equal force to internal evaluation, conducted by members of the school staff, critical friends or pupils. OFSTED's guidelines for self-evaluation see this as the responsibility of heads of department and headteachers. The 1999 *School Teachers' Pay and Conditions* document includes among the duties of the head: 'Evaluating the standards of teaching and learning in the school and ensuring that proper standards of professional performance are established and maintained' (DFEE (1999), para. 43.7).

Headteachers are in some senses 'external' evaluators of teaching. Although advised by OFSTED not to play the role of internal inspectors, their presence can also be seen as threatening and 'high stakes' by the teacher. The head's advantage over the inspector is the knowledge of school and community that she brings with her. Heads are in a better position to contextualise what they see both in terms of the school as a whole and in terms of that individual teacher's developmental history. They not only bring some prior knowledge, however, but preconceptions and prejudices, so that their lines of sight will inevitably differ from those of the more 'neutral' visitor who is less familiar with the school. These advantages and disadvantages need to be acknowledged and balanced. The more 'upfront' headteachers are about the purpose and protocol of the visit, the more negotiated the process, the more open and supportive the feedback, the less will be the threat and the greater the returns for both parties.

The starting point is with the teacher herself, with her own evaluation of her teaching which can be placed alongside that of the observer, so providing a basis for dialogue and negotiation. The teacher, from her vantage point, will see and understand things the observer neither sees nor understands, while from the observer's vantage point there are things invisible to the teacher. So, observation or evaluation schedules can be most useful and productive if completed by the teacher herself as well as by the visiting observer.

This has assumed higher stakes with threshold assessments in England which allow teachers to receive bonus pay if they meet a set of criteria. These provide the starting point for the teacher's own evaluation (Figure 3.2).

Whether such high-stakes assessment is conducive to honest self-appraisal is another matter. But this set of criteria may serve a double function: one private, the other public. Before going public it may be a useful rehearsal to invite a critical friend to have his or her say. There is an Irish saying *Is maith an scathan suil carad*, which is, in translation: 'A good mirror is the eye of a friend.'

- Have a thorough and up-to-date knowledge of the teaching of their subject(s) and take account of wider curriculum developments which are relevant to their work;
- Consistently and effectively plan lessons and sequences of lessons to meet pupils' individual learning needs;
- Consistently and effectively use a range of appropriate strategies for teaching and classroom management;
- Consistently and effectively use information about minor attainment to set well-grounded expectations for pupils and monitor progress to give clear and constructive feedback;
- Show that, as a result of their teaching, their pupils achieve well relative to the pupils' prior attainment, making progress as good as or better than similar pupils nationally;
- Take responsibility for their professional development and use the outcomes to improve their teaching and pupils' learning;
- Make an active contribution to the policies and aspirations of the school.

Figure 3.2 Threshold criteria

The role of the pupil

Much of the evaluation literature assumes that observation of teaching is the province of those in a position of higher authority than the teacher: inspectors, headteachers, heads of department. While headteachers are ultimately accountable for the performance of the school (a high-stakes issue for them), assuring the quality of learning and teaching does not necessarily imply direct first-hand observation.

The most informed sources on the qualities of teachers tend to be ritually ignored, that is the pupils. Pupils are rarely mentioned as evaluators even though they have the most intimate knowledge of their teachers' strengths and weaknesses. Many of the published self-evaluation questionnaires skate circumspectly around the issues, posing general questions as to pupil satisfaction with teaching but rarely asking for a direct comment on specific teachers.

There are sound ethical reasons for this. Systematic collection of pupil evaluations by senior management can be divisive and inimical to the ethos of trust that is the hallmark of the good school and classroom.

However, there are excellent examples of pupil evaluations being used sensitively and formatively within a trusting environment. One such example comes from a German school which took part in a self-evaluation project organised by the Bertelsmann Foundation (2000). Schwalmstadt Schule in Hesse devised a questionnaire which asked pupils to evaluate their teachers on twenty specific criteria. These are shown in Figure 3.3:

Being assessed by their classes was entirely a voluntary activity for teachers. However, 78% took part and a total of 107 surveys were collected and aggregated to school level. Each teacher had a code number known only to herself so that the evaluations could serve two benefits: one for the teacher herself and the other for the school as a whole. The aggregated results show across the school as a whole where the strengths and weaknesses in teaching lie, data which provide a useful platform for professional development. More useful, though, is the use

---

My teacher prepares his lessons quite well.

My teacher uses a variety of teaching methods.

His/her teaching is clear and understandable.

I feel I am learning.

Tests are given back on time.

My teacher has a good knowledge of his/her subject.

His/her teaching is boring/lively/inspiring.

He/she is quite 'human'.

She/he has a good sense of humour.

He/she starts lessons on time.

He/she accepts us as individuals and is interested in our problems.

She/he puts pressure on us to work well.

He/she ignores us when we put up our hands.

He/she makes use of our contributions.

She/he shows that she values what we have to say.

She/he tries to involve all pupils in the lesson.

He/she is fair in his/her marking.

She/he is open to criticism and does not pretend to be perfect.

Her/his class management leads to unrest.

I would like to have this teacher again next year.

Figure 3.3 Items from the German questionnaire

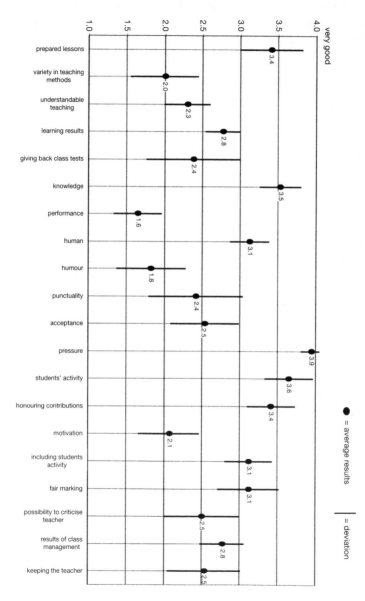

Figure 3.4 Evaluation: learning and teaching

of these data at the level of the individual teacher (Figure 3.4). When the teacher gets this feedback it is not to be taken simply at face value but taken as a fruitful point of departure for deeper probing. The teacher whose class generated the data shown in Figure 3.4 chose to present these to his pupils and to ask for their help in interpreting the figures. It won him an immediate accolade from the class and produced rich rewards. It led to the recognition that the quality of teaching is not simply down to the efforts and ability of the teacher but a shared responsibility in which pupils have considerable power and influence. They can be helped to exercise this to shape the quality of teaching as well as the quality of learning.

The range of variance, represented by the vertical lines in the graph, tells its own story. It illustrates how different can be the perceptions of the 'same' teacher and how large those differences can be, because they are experienced quite differently depending on relationships and pupils' prior history. For example, listening to pupils and respecting their opinions is not a single measurable attribute of a teacher. Teachers do not treat all pupils 'the same'. They discriminate. They value some contributions (and contributors) more than others. Pupils are much more sensitive to this than their teachers. They have not only the history of this one teacher to colour their judgement but a history of years of teachers and years of judgements about their personal value and value relative to their classsmates.

We may have to travel some way before we establish such an open self-critical climate in our schools. Such transparency may not sit easily with performance management, but nor is there a necessary contradiction. Teachers who have collected this kind of feedback on a systematic basis from their pupils for their own professional development purposes can include such data in their own portfolios and submission for above-the-threshold payments.

What these evaluations showed very clearly was the ability of school pupils to make discriminating judgements and to be measured and fair in doing so. A word of caution to inspectorates embarking on a more systematic collection of pupil views of their school. Pupils will be very honest when they are sure of the purpose as a formative one. They may be less forthcoming when their views are to be used as an accountability tool. As we have repeatedly discovered, pupils can be very loyal to their school and their teachers when the stakes are high. Evidence from a recent case study (Dannaway, 2001) of the private and public faces of pupils is discussed in chapter 7.

Who should evaluate teaching?

When we consider the range of possible evaluators all have their own advantages and drawbacks. Figure 3.6 suggests some of these. It is however difficult to generalise as so much depends on the individual, the school, the community, and teachers' and pupils' prior experience of inspection or self-evaluation. The way in which evaluation of teaching is presented to staff – as an opportunity or threat, a burden or a benefit – will be a crucial factor in determining how effectively evaluators will do their job.

Thinking of your own school, how would you describe the pluses and minuses of each of the following kinds of observers?

inspectors
the headteacher
the head of department
a colleague chosen by yourself
a colleague chosen at random
pupils
a researcher

Figure 3.5 A class evaluates its teacher

We might describe some of the possible pluses and minuses of each in the following way:

Plus	*Minus*
The inspector Connoisseurship Training Prior experience Authority	Lack of time High stakes Lack of contextual knowledge
The headteacher Informal knowledge Authority	Limited time Fairly high stakes Relatively little experience
The teaching colleague Trust Negotiation Reciprocity Knowledge of context	Limited time Limited expertise
The teacher herself/himself Self knowledge Familiarity with the class as individuals Knowledge of context	Familiarity Protection of ego
The pupil Day-to-day knowledge Motivation Time	Lack of authority Little expertise Overfamiliarity

Figure 3.6 Who evaluates – pluses and minuses

Power, expertise and validity

Another way of thinking about the various players and their impact is in terms of three continua on which they may be placed. For example, on the power continuum, inspectors are firmly at the high (ten out of ten) end while pupils are at the other. On the expertise continuum inspectors will in most (but not all) cases be at the high end with most (but not all) pupils at the lower end.

The power continuum

| 0 | pupils | teachers | governors | headteacher | inspectors | 10 |

The expertise continuum

| 0 | pupils | governors | teachers | headteacher | inspectors | 10 |

On the third continuum – the validity of the evaluation – the question is much more open to discussion.

QUESTION:

Thinking of your own school and perhaps recent experience of self-evaluation and/or inspection, where would you place the various players on the validity continuum?

The validity continuum

0   10

Validity in evaluation of teaching is what we seek above all because what are at stake are the reputation, status, confidence and morale of the teacher. Without these it is futile to talk about raising standards in our schools.

4 Evaluating learning

Intelligence is 'knowing what to do when you don't know what to do.' – Piaget.

The evaluation of learning comes at the issues from a quite different direction from the evaluation of teaching. Its starting point is with the individual pupil, with her life experience, and with learning defined in its broadest sense. It encompasses her attitudes to school, to teachers, to learning, to self. It is concerned with self-definition and how an individual gives meaning to what she experiences as 'learning' – in the home, community, school and classroom. It recognises the importance of the peer group and the power it has to shape individual attitudes, motivation and achievement.

When we start with evaluation in this very broad experiential context we deepen our understanding of how individual pupils interpret and internalise what the teacher is teaching. In Judith Little's words (1990), we adopt an attitude of 'aggressive curiosity and healthy scepticism' as to the relationship between what is taught and what is learned.

There is also, as Watkins (2001) points out, a difference between a learning and a performance orientation. Measurement that is impelled by a competitive, league-table way of thinking leads to a set of beliefs and attitudes which may be at odds with deep learning or learning how to learn. In a sense we may describe these as contrasting approaches: one from the outside in and the other from the inside out.

The more we try to understand the individual child 'from the inside' the more we find out that we need to frame classroom events in different

Learning orientation	*Performance orientation*
Belief that effort leads to success	Belief that ability leads to success
Belief in one's ability to improve and learn	Concern to be judged as able, concern to perform
Preference for challenging tasks	Satisfaction from doing better than others
Derives satisfaction from personal success at difficult tasks	Emphasis on normative standards, competition and public evaluation
Uses self-instruction when engaged in task	Helplessness: evaluate self negatively when task is difficult

Figure 4.1 Comparing a learning and a performance orientation (Watkins, 2001)

ways. We no longer try to see things 'as they are' because there is no singular reality. A classroom may be both a comfortable place and a terrifying one, constructive and destructive. depending from where it is viewed. For the evaluator, of course, this poses a complex, and even awesome, task, but one of critical importance because it helps us to arrive at a more inclusive appreciation of how children learn and how differently they do so.

While the evaluation of teaching has drawn heavily on research into school and teacher effectiveness, the evaluation of individual learning has looked to cognitive and social psychology. It attempts to probe individual thinking and feeling and how the learner 'constructs' his learning. It sets this not just in the formal classroom context but also in the context of home, through 'homework' and study, and in relationship with others who mediate learning: parents, peers, friends, mentors, private tutors.

While a daunting task there are a number of ways in which this can be undertaken, ranging from the simple and obvious to the highly sophisticated and technical. One simple, easy-to-use strategy is to find a few minutes in the ongoing life of the classroom for the teacher to stand back from the lesson and reflect on three basic questions:

- What are the pupils doing?
- What are they learning?
- What am I doing?

To this may be added a fourth, formative, question, 'What am I going to do next?' This exercise is obviously best undertaken when pupils are engaged in some activity and the teacher is free to observe.

The answer to the question 'What are they doing?' may have a simple reply: writing in their books. But a little deeper probing might reveal some more complex and varied activity: some writing, some copying from their neighbour, some stuck and looking for help. Probing a little deeper may reveal that pupil activities are rarely singular or linear. That is, they tend not to engage in one activity at a time nor to move in a neat sequence from one activity to the next. Pupil behaviour tends to be of a more random and simultaneous nature.

Learning is embedded within the social context of teachers and peers, past histories, friendships, rivalries, secret lives whose public faces teachers and inspectors are not allowed to penetrate. Without access to inner emotions and thoughts we can only use proxy measures. We can only have access to the products of thinking which may, in truth, be pale reflections of the inner life of children's minds.

So one good starting point, advocated by OFSTED, is to examine children's work.

Evaluating the product

How much can a visiting observer tell from a single piece of work? A limited amount, without seeing that work in a context over time, in relation to the child's endeavours in other curricular areas and in relation to the work of others in the same class. To a practised eye this may reveal much, but deeper understanding may require further probing. An essay, a poem, a drawing, a mathematical solution may be used as a starting point for a dialogue with the pupil, helping him to articulate what brought him to that end point. A further useful technique is to use what is called a 'think-aloud protocol' whereby the researcher, teacher or mentor sits beside the pupil and asks her to talk aloud about what she is doing and thinking while engaging in a piece of work. The advantages and pitfalls of such an approach are described in a fascinating study by Lings and Desforges (1999).

When an external observer, or the classroom teacher, engages in such inquiry that person comes to see what is before them less as an inert product and more as a living and evolving expression of a child's inner life. Teachers are sometimes shocked to find the misconceptions that students are working on and the erroneous assumptions they have made. On the other hand, they are sometimes shocked to discover their own misconceptions and snap judgements.

Ted Wragg tells the story about the teacher who had asked the class to draw a head and shoulders. All but one dutifully produced a conventional portrait, face on or in profile. The one exception, however, was the pupil who had covered the sheet with a bands of vivid colour, nothing like a head and shoulders – at least to the casual observer or to the irate teacher who might interpret this as an act of defiance or vandalism. With a little patient probing the pupil was able to explain that this was indeed a head but 'seen from the inside'.

In Coalsnaughton Primary School, the seven class teachers meet round the table to examine examples of children's work. Each of the teachers has brought one example from her own class. Each piece of work is discussed for five to ten minutes, teachers giving their own judgements as to the quality of the work. They do not always agree, but summative evaluation is not the primary purpose. They are seeking to broaden their understanding through discussion of the child, the context of his work, and his progression and growth.

In St Kentigern's Academy, ten teachers, each from different subject departments, discuss the work and behaviour of one individual pupil. Each brings a different perception of Eric's behaviour and ability. He is clearly not the 'same' boy in PE as he is in maths. His relationship with his geography teacher is markedly different from his relationship with his science teacher. While the staff come to a greater understanding of Eric 'in the round', they also gain a deeper insight into themselves and set their teaching in a broader social and psychological context.

QUESTIONS:

What strategies do you use to get a broader picture of pupils' work?
What strategies might you initiate or develop?

What did you learn at school today?

We may try to answer the learning question in a direct way by simply asking pupils 'What did you learn?' This is a useful question because it challenges the pupil to reflect on what he or she has taken away from a day, a period, or a ten-minute episode, not simply in terms of an item of content taught but in terms of the impact and meaning it has for him or her. The answer does, however, require the intellectual and verbal tools for the pupil to be able to perceive and then articulate what has been learned. Even experienced adults can find this a difficult question to answer. Nonetheless, answers can often be illuminating, even from very young children. They can often reveal amusing and disturbing conceptions of what learning is and what it is for. Most importantly, though, the question can set off a quest into language and meaning and begin to build a linguistic and conceptual toolkit for the learner.

Adding a little structure to the question may help (Figure 4.1). Such open-ended instruments do generate a lot of data and if done on a large scale can be incredibly time-consuming. Feedback of this kind is likely to be most useful in the hands of the classroom teacher with a specific formative purpose.

As more structure is added the need for open-ended comment becomes less. So, as in the example in Figure 4.2, data become more quantifiable while still leaving room for individual comment.

Even more sophisticated is the 'subjective experience sampling' used by two American researchers, Leone and Richards (1989). During one week they paged pupils at random intervals between 7.30 a.m. and 9.30 p.m., asking them to complete a simple rating scale to indicate their feeling, motivation, arousal at that particular moment. While this is perhaps too sophisticated for a school to undertake there are simpler variations on the theme.

The spot check

The 'spot check' is a one-page sheet containing 14 paired items, for example:

Anxious/relaxed
Active/passive
Difficult to concentrate/easy to concentrate
Wishing to be here/wishing to be somewhere else

Before you start the lesson, please circle the word(s) most relevant to you:

too cold   too hot   happy   sad   lethargic   bored   excited   tired   hungry   angry   scared

Tick or colour in one of the faces below to show your level of interest in what you are about to learn:

SPOT CHECK

concentrating	1	2	3	thinking about other things
alert	1	2	3	drowsy
relaxed	1	2	3	anxious
wishing to be here	1	2	3	wishing to be somewhere else
happy	1	2	3	sad
active	1	2	3	passive
excited	1	2	3	bored
time passing quickly	1	2	3	time passing slowly
full of energy	1	2	3	very little energy
something at stake	1	2	3	nothing at stake
sociable	1	2	3	lonely
easy to concentrate	1	2	3	difficult to concentrate
cheerful	1	2	3	irritable
easy to be creative	1	2	3	difficult to be creative

At the end of the lesson tick or colour in one of the faces below to show what you feel you have benefited from the lesson:

Figure 4.2 The spot check

It asks pupils to take a minute, or less, to fill out it at a given moment such as a signal from the teacher or the sound of an alarm clock . A three- or four-point scale may be used so that there are intermediate responses between anxious and relaxed, for example. Like Leone and Richards' pager, its greatest benefit will come from using it across a range of contexts and times of day. For example, what might we learn about different levels of motivation and thinking when a pupil is:

• Listening to the teacher in a geography lesson
• Engaged in role play in drama
• Reading a book in the library
• Looking for information on the Net
• Doing mathematics homework
• Watching *Neighbours* on television
• Studying for a test while listening to music
• Reading a *Harry Potter* book in bed

The spot check is a way of ascertaining at any given moment what is happening, not in the observable external behavioural world but in the internal behavioural world of thinking and feeling. As some philosophers and sociologists are fond of telling us, there is no such thing as the present and we can at best only capture what immediately preceded the inter-vention of the spot check. So the spot check is, in a sense, like lifting a single frame from a moving picture at a totally arbitrary moment but in doing so offering intriguing interpretations of what went before and what might come after.

An adaptation of the spot check was used in a very innovative project called the Learning School. Their adaptation of the spot-check instru-ment is shown in Figure 4.2.

The Learning School, the global classroom

The Learning School project involved groups of students from seven schools: in Scotland, Sweden, the Czech Republic, Germany, Japan, South Korea and South Africa. The students, who each took a year out of school for their global classroom journey, spent up to six weeks in each of the participating schools evaluating the quality of learning and teaching, school ethos and pupils' differing individual experience of

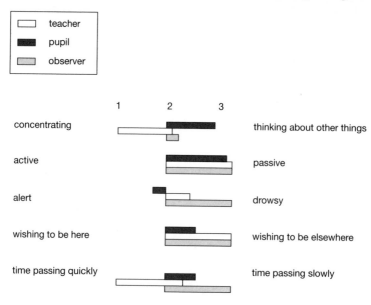

Figure 4.3 Examples of pupil, teacher and observer ratings on the spot check

school and classroom life. They used a number of different methodologies including observation, shadowing, interviewing and spot checks. At each stage of their journey (geographical and educational) they reported back their tentative findings for the scrutiny of teachers and other students and also, at given points, to academics, researchers, inspectors and policy-makers. Finally in Japan at the end of June a week-long conference was held to present findings to various international audiences including staff and students from the participating schools.

The Learning School students introduced a compelling variation on the spot check, a 'triangulation' of three different viewpoints: pupil, teacher and student observer. At a given moment in the class lesson all three parties filled out the spot check sheet, the teacher and observer making a judgement about the whole class, the pupil giving his or her own individual response. Aggregating all pupil responses with that of the teacher and observer gave an intriguing picture of quite different perceptions of what was happening in one classroom (Figure 4.3).

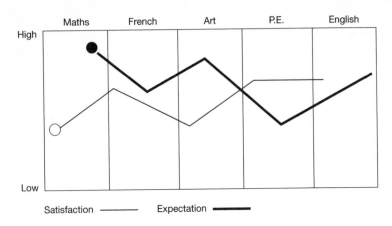

Figure 4.4 Comparison of expectation and satisfaction

What does the teacher then do with this ambiguous information? He or she may dismiss it as worthless or may choose to engage with her class in a deeper exploration of what the data mean and where they may point in respect of future practice. Without this, the data are relatively meaningless, if rather sobering. With an open mind and willingness to embark on an exciting journey of discovery, the class may, as Guy Claxton (2000) suggests, transform perplexity into mastery:

> Learning starts from the joint acknowledgement of inadequacy and ignorance . . . There is no other place for learning to start. An effective learner, or learning culture, is one that is not afraid to admit this perception, and also possesses some confidence in its ability to grow in understanding and expertise, so that perplexity is transformed into mastery . . .

The expectation and satisfaction graph

A further intriguing offshoot of this was a simple litmus test of pupils' expectations and engagement over the course of one day. Pupils were asked to record their expectation of a lesson at the beginning and then their engagement/level of satisfaction at the end. As Figure 4.4 reveals, expectation can sometimes exceed satisfaction and low expectation can sometimes be surprised into achievement.

A further refinement of this, as illustrated in Figure 4.5, is the graph of engagement over one single period. Based on a spot check every ten minutes the graph shows when the pupil is more and less engaged with what is happening in the class.

The value of these data was limited, however, without the further exploration through talking and explaining and seeking to get inside the pupil's experience. So the Learning School researchers would sit down with a pupil and probe some of the inner feelings that provoked the completion of the spot check or the expectation/satisfaction graph. The following is an extract from one of those follow-up sessions – ten minutes or less – but exploiting the immediacy of the experience and the power of present feeling.

The Learning School project was able to get beneath the skin of individual pupil's classroom experience through a combination of shadowing, spot checks and interviews taken together and in complement. It highlights the importance of the relationship between data-gatherer and data source combined with the facilitative and probing skills of the well-constructed and sensitively conducted interview.

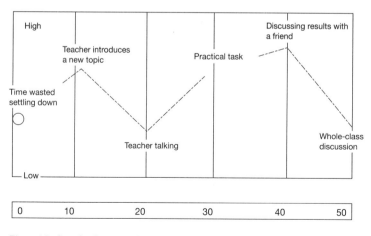

Figure 4.5 Graph of one pupil's engagement over a fifty-minute period

Reporting on thinking

A study by Luan (1997) in Singapore followed a similar path, asking
students to report on their thinking during a series of lessons. These data
were then desegregated according to the ability level of the student,
revealing the pattern shown in Table 4.1.

The results are intriguing but perhaps raise more questions than they
answer.

QUESTION:

Before proceeding further, what questions do these results raise for
you?

Analysing further to try and identify the quality of thinking taking place
during the lesson, yet more intriguing leads were suggested (Table 4.2).

On the face of it, it would appear that high-ability students were
less likely to pay attention, and (as the first table suggested) more likely
to engage in lesson-irrelevant thinking. The general failure to use higher-
order thinking skills is apparent among all groups.

Table 4.1 Evaluating relevant thinking – by ability

	Low ability		Average ability		High ability	
	n	%	n	%	n	%
Not thinking actively	139	39.5	169	24.2	128	20.2
Lesson-irrelevant thinking	88	22.4	196	28.0	262	41.3
Lesson-relevant and irrelevant thinking	18	4.6	44	6.3	77	12.1
Lesson-relevant thinking	147	37.5	290	41.5	167	26.3

Source: (Luan, p. 193)

Table 4.2 What pupils were doing – by ability group

	Low ability		Average ability		High ability	
	n	*%*	*n*	*%*	*n*	*%*
Note-taking	7	1.8	9	1.3	98	15.5
Paying attention	321	98.2	547	78.7	406	64.3
Responding to questions	19	4.8	44	6.3	25	3.9
Trying to understand	165	42.1	334	47.8	245	38.6
Visualising	10	2.5	47	6.7	33	5.2
Assimilating	21	5.4	27	3.9	27	4.3
Applying	7	1.8	12	1.7	9	1.4
Hypothesising	3	0.8	14	2.0	8	1.3
Analysing	16	4.1	38	5.4	54	8.5
Evaluating	11	2.8	16	2.3	125	3.9

Source: (Luan, p. 195)

QUESTIONS:

What you might deduce from this second table?
Are there suggestive lines of inquiry here?
Could this be adapted for use in your school or classroom as a self-evaluation tool?

The results are surprising and difficult to interpret as they stand. They require some qualitative information to help make sense of them. This was carried out in this study through interviews with students about their self-reports. The following statements give important clues to the meaning of the quantitative data (Luan, p. 196):

'It was very detailed. The teacher used confusing terms. My friends asked "deep" questions beyond what the teacher taught . . . I get very frustrated because everyone else seems to understand.'

'I was distracted and could not concentrate.'

'I was troubled with problems I had.'

'I wasn't thinking of any stuff at that time because I was concentrating on writing the notes. I mean it is not easy to write and listen for I can only do one thing at a time.'

'The teacher's voice and expression can be very dull at times. I think tone and expression play a great part in helping students understand the lesson better.'

These are thought-provoking comments. As in the case of the spot check we discover something about students' mental absenteeism. We are not surprised to find they are worrying about problems located elsewhere. We are, perhaps, more disturbed to find that taking notes seems to be divorced from thinking. Does it point to a certain kind of note-taking skill or, as the failure of higher-order thinking suggests, a lack of training in the ability to abstract personal meaning from teacher talk?

As was mentioned in a previous chapter, we have to exercise caution when it comes to 'verbal data' and self-reporting, especially when it is in retrospect. It must also be borne in mind that it also requires of students some high-level language skills as well as conceptual skills. The data may, therefore, be regarded as 'soft' and tentative. But from a teacher's, as opposed to a researcher's, point of view, it provides a good base for exploratory dialogue with students and is useful as a way of introducing them to a higher level of self-analysis, or 'metacognitive' activity. This can be an invaluable strategy for teachers to use in their own classrooms and to help students monitor their own learning.

Pupil voice: uses and abuses

How and what we gather by way of pupil data is a sensitive issue not simply for teachers but for pupils too. In explaining our purposes to them what rationale do we give and how honest are we? Michael Fielding (1999) suggests four levels at which we gather student views:

- Pupils as data source
- Pupils as active respondents

- Pupils as co-researchers
- Pupils as researchers

In evaluating learning these distinctions become critical because they signal our purposes. In school-effectiveness research the most common use of student voice is as a data source, informing researchers about the quality or effectiveness of the school. Some school improvement approaches take a further step, feeding back data and engaging pupils more actively in dialogue with a purpose which tries to get to grips with the interpretation of the data by pupils themselves (see for example Figure 3.4). When pupils become co-researchers they enter more actively into the process from the start, sharing ownership with teachers or researchers. This would be true of evaluation strategies in which pupils played a part in the design of questionnaires, discussed processes of data gathering and analysis and felt they had a real stake in what was happening. The fourth category is one which allows students a great deal of responsibility and authority for driving the process. This would be exemplified well by the Learning School project in which teachers and headteachers played a subsidiary role.

Work currently underway on the Economic and Social Research Council's teaching and learning programme is identifying ways of consulting pupils about their learning and helping schools to be more receptive to the pupil voice. The network builds on ground-breaking work by Jean Rudduck (1995), Michael Fielding, Madeleine Arnot, Diane Reay (1998), Kate Myers (2000) and others on pupil voice, work which has taken us a long way in understanding how pupils construct their knowledge, form their identity as learners and apply labels to themselves as 'bright', 'clever' or 'stupid'. It probes more deeply into the how of learning and the identity of learners.

Pupils as co-researchers

When pupils are engaged as co-researchers, they become even more active collaborators in understanding learning and generating new knowledge.

Teachers who are willing to listen sensitively and non-defensively to their pupils not only enhance their relationship with the class but become better teachers.

Fielding's fourth category (pupils as researchers) describes initiatives taken by pupils themselves leading the dialogue, engaging with their peers and with their teachers in order to deepen their understanding of learning and the contexts of learning. This may be exemplified by some of the initiatives taken by pupils in the Socrates Project, 'Evaluating Quality in School Education' (MacBeath et al., 1998).

In a Swedish school, one of the participating English school students equipped with a tape recorder dropped into classes at random around the school and also at random picked a student to question about his or her learning at that moment, recording the data to allow later analysis of the whole sample.

One of the most revealing aspects of the spot check and the Leone and Richards (1989) pager experiment is in spotlighting the context of learning and its critical influence on how well we learn. One thing we are becoming more and more aware of is the power of place. Everyone has their own favourite place for relaxing, working, being creative. As adults we attend lectures, sit through sermons, film and theatre, with our concentration span determined not just by the quality of the presentation but by the temperature of the room, light and colour, the comfort of the seats, the people we are with, our level of hunger or thirst, our previous patterns of sleep.

We sometimes appear to assume that children are oblivious to these contextual effects. We expect that children will sit still on uncomfortable wooden seats for hours on end absorbing information in tranquillity and passivity, in drab and barren rooms, sometimes too hot and sometimes too cold, poorly lit and ventilated.

Learning out of school

What do children and young people do when left to their own devices? What do they do when left to create their own environment for learning? This was one of the questions we sought to answer when we started our research into homework in the late 1980s. We visited homes and talked to parents and their children about how they set about their study and homework, how they made choices. These interviews often gave us the chance to observe children at work, in front of the TV, listening to their Walkmans, on the phone to their friends, helping younger sisters or older brothers, teaching or getting support from a friendly teddy bear. What we learned from this was just how different individuals are not just in terms of how they learn but the physical and social contexts where that learning takes place.

Advice by schools to young people and their parents often betrayed a lack of understanding of the real world of children's home learning. Advice to pupils and parents typically advocated a quiet place to work, a desk and a desk light, an upright chair, a place free from interruptions. Few young people worked to that pattern, vending their own most comfortable, convenient and often corner-cutting style. What was most comfortable was psychologically important, but it was not always the most efficient or effective. This led us to two conclusions. One, that we should understand more and accommodate more to different home and family contexts and to the individuality of the learner. Two, that within that comfort zone young people could benefit a great deal from help in making their work more economical, more efficient and more enjoyable.

We were also convinced by our observations in classrooms and homes that to separate out 'homework' as a discrete phenomenon, separate and distinct from other kinds of learning, was a mistake. It reinforced a view of learning as something that happens in school, directed by teachers, and homework as some dutiful piece of busywork to be completed and got out of the way as rapidly as possible. There was a hiatus between classwork and homework. Classroom learning was often stimulating and inventive; pupils worked in pairs and groups and discussed and shared what they were doing. In the evening, work at home did not have that same impetus and homework tasks rarely seemed to give the same thought to the needs and context of the learner nor to coherence and progression of learning.

We asked young people to keep a detailed log for one week documenting what they did, who with, and how long they spent on it. We also asked them to record their feelings, their completion or incompletion of the task and their level of frustration or satisfaction. It was clear from the logs that many young people invested huge amounts of time on ineffective, unfocused copying or reading, struggling to make their own sense of the printed page or giving up at the first hurdle. Often there was little visible payoff in return for the time and emotional energy invested.

Young people were often encouraged to plan their time over the week, a timetable beforehand, a routine of work in the early evening or after school. These admonitions failed to reflect the reality of young people's lives. Like adults, young people worked in a variety of ways and places and at times which suited their domestic routines or personal biorhythms, or fitted the geography and social composition of the home.

Something like half the sample of pupils worked against a background of loud music. They eventually persuaded initially sceptical researchers that it actually helped them to concentrate. It created a sound barrier between them and the outside distractions of half-heard conversations, television, phones and doorbells ringing, parents and siblings arguing. Parents' graphic descriptions of opening the bedroom door to find their child 'sitting behind a wall of noise' was a piece of convincing imagery. Some pupils described how distracting the utter silence of a library could be when each shuffle and drop of a pencil became resounding events.

The response from schools to the publication of the study demonstrated clearly that homework was seen both as important but also as a contentious and complex issue for teachers and school management. Many of the issues raised seemed to touch the very heart of learning and teaching and could only be addressed through long-term development and a change of expectations on the part of teachers, parents and pupils.

The question that intrigued us was: how much of what pupils did for their homework fed directly into their thinking and memory, remaining with them as significant and meaningful learning which they could retrieve and use at a later date? In other words, how much of it enriched the mental structuring of knowledge? attitudes to the subject in question or learning in general? or skills that could be applied in some real-life situation?

Making homework work

The success, or otherwise, of homework and home study could be put down to some key factors: three at the in-school end and three at the out-of-school end:

In school

- Clear formulation, communication and discussion of the task by the teacher
- Establishing patterns, timing and distribution of work within the school as a whole
- Using homework as a bridge between learning in and out of school

Out of school

- Clarity of purpose and continuity of the task
- Support, reinforcement and feedback at critical points
- Coaching in strategies for effective learning

Some of these factors could be addressed relatively easily. Homework could be communicated more effectively, not as an afterthought while the bell was ringing and pupils were exiting the classroom both mentally and physically. It could be planned and integrated into courses in advance rather than used as a finishing-off of class work, a still common practice not only iniquitous but suggestive of bad planning and lack of differentiation. Primary schools could build some progression up through the school, and secondary schools could ensure some horizontal co-ordination across different departments.

Study support

Study support, homework clubs and other forms of out-of-hours learning, have been a high government priority under New Labour, with Lottery money being channelled to schools through the New Opportunities Fund. The location of study centres in football clubs, Playing for Success, has been seen widely as highly successful and the national evaluation of study support showed significant added-value. For teachers and pupils one of the most conspicuous benefits was learning to work in a context entirely different from the conventional classroom. The voluntary nature of attendance, the informal teacher-pupil relationships, the relaxed ethos, the student-centred nature of the learning, all combined to make learning more accessible and more enjoyable for many pupils who had struggled in the more competitive controlled classroom environment.

When we evaluate learning in that context we open the door to new understanding about where, how, when and with whom pupils learn best and how different 'best' learning can be. The National Codes of Practice for primary and secondary schools and for libraries offer useful guidelines and probing questions for the evaluation of study support.

In conclusion

As Descartes discovered in his celebrated proof of our higher-order existence, we are the only species capable of thinking about our thinking or thinking about our being. The more we know about our intellectual tools and how to use them the more effective we can become as learners and as teachers. The more we understand about our own emotional and moral responses the more meaningful our thinking becomes. As teachers we need to be able to consider how confidently we can answer these questions:

- How much do we encourage students to experiment with learning, to discover their bent as visual, auditory, or kinaesthetic learners?
- How aware are they of their own profile of intelligences?
- Do we encourage them to try out different places for homework, study and home learning?
- How can we carry over these insights into the school and classroom context?
- To what extent do they realise for themselves the significance of learning skills for their present and future lives?

5 Evaluating ethos and culture

While we recognise that the ethos and culture of a school are the groundbed of all that takes place within the organisation, these often get bypassed in formal evaluations of quality and standards. This is because ethos and culture are not only difficult to measure but even difficult to define. Yet everything in our experience tells us that these are crucial factors in home or institutional life. Whether we are talking about schools, colleges, hospitals, hotels or restaurants, the homes we visit or the homes we live in, we are highly sensitive to the climate or ethos whose impact on us is immediate. First impressions count and tend to linger. But how can this impact be described in more objective terms than the feeling we get when go through the front door?

If 'ethos', 'climate' or 'culture' are to be treated seriously and systematically in the evaluation of schools, the first imperative is to be clear about terminology and concepts. The second task is to probe deeper to discover how these things come about, how they are created and sustained and how they can be changed. The third task is to examine what part ethos and culture play in both internal and external evaluation.

A matter of definition?

The terms 'ethos' and 'culture' tend to be used synonymously, but it is useful to make a distinction between the two. Per Dalin (1993) describes 'ethos' as the outward, or surface, expression of a school's norms and values which lie more deeply buried in the 'culture' of the organisation. This deeper-lying organisational culture is less easy to perceive and more elusive to the casual visitor. It is a phenomenon, as its name suggests, which has gestated over time and taken on a life of its own.

So we may describe ethos in terms of the first impressions one has as a visitor: the feel of the school, the environment (light, colour, warmth, displays of work. welcoming posters). It may also be expressed in the personal aspects: the welcome of office staff, the helpfulness of the care-taker, the positive attitude of teachers and pupils, the subliminal smile index. These are all, to some extent, measurable, although to reduce ethos to these simple discrete elements may do violence to the whole in which all of these things work together to create something greater than the sum of the parts.

Underlying this surface manifestation of goodwill – or wind chill – is the culture of the school. It is composed of values and beliefs, feelings and attitudes, relationships (pupil-to-pupil, teacher-to-teacher, pupil-teacher) and the taken-for-granted way in which all of these parties go about their daily business. So while it may be possible to create a certain superficial ethos, often in the weeks prior to an inspection visit, culture has a longer history and deeper roots. And while an initially welcoming ethos may fool the casual visitor, it is an illusion difficult to sustain over time. Just as a troubled individual may present a pleasing face to the world, so can an organisation; but it strains credibility to believe that a truly welcoming and vibrant ethos could in fact conceal a troubled and conflicted culture.

Culture has been described as 'the way we do things round here'. It is a powerful social adhesive, held in place by the norms, language, beliefs, roles and day-to-day relationships of teachers and pupils, promoted and unpromoted staff, teachers and parents. 'The way we do things round here' is illustrated in the following account of a new teacher taking up a first post in a Scottish secondary school in the 1960s:

> I was determined not to use the belt, but in taking that stance was the only teacher in the school who refused to use it. Hardly a day went by when I wasn't exhorted by colleagues to join the real world and recognise that pupils expected it and that good order could not be promoted without this sanction. It was about a month into my teaching when I had to capitulate and visit the staffroom to borrow a belt from one of my colleagues. It provided a general cause for celebration. It was expressed by one member of staff as 'another young teacher loses his idealism'. I had become a welcomed member of the school staff – one of the boys.

A decade later, 'the way we do things round here' is never to use corporal punishment, and a decade after that it came to be seen as virtually unthinkable and barbaric. A book written in the late 1960s about Harlem schools provides a further illustration of the power of the cultural status quo. Entitled *The Way it Spozed to Be* (Herndon, 1968) the book recounts a teacher's vain attempts to change pupils' expectations of relationships and of learning. Sadly, shaking their heads, pupils had to advise their teacher, Mister Herndon, that his attempts to change things did not accord with 'the way it spozed to be'. As James Herndon found, cultures can be powerful inhibitors of change. However, the good news is that cultures can also be change-friendly, innovative, risk-taking and open to new ideas.

The roots of culture

The culture of a school is developed through the history that each individual or group brings to the school. Even a brand-new school has a powerful past. While the bricks and mortar may be new, the school nonetheless has a history, contained in the prior experiences that each individual brings. This means that several cultures or sub-cultures may exist within a school: among different groups of young people, among different sets of staff and among parents. The values and norms of these separate subcultures may be coherent or incongruent, with quite different implications for the school and its improvement. These will express themselves at many different levels, from the individual level through to the interface of school and community (see Figure 5.1).

There is a rich and extensive literature on micro cultures within schools, each bounded by gender, race, class, ability, pro and anti-school, conformist and 'delinquescent' (Hargreaves (1967), Willis (1977), Mirza (1992), Arnott, (2001)). It is beyond the scope of inspection to capture the turbulent dynamic of these cultures or their complex layers of interrelationship. Sensitive self-evaluation can shed light on the differential experiences of children, their affiliations and identities, but may require the support and expertise of an external critical friend to probe beneath the hidden curricula, guarded reticences and institutional inhibitions.

Such probing may reveal different perceptions of equality and inclusivity. Do pupils feel equally valued? Do they have equal access to resources material and human – to the richest resources of the school,

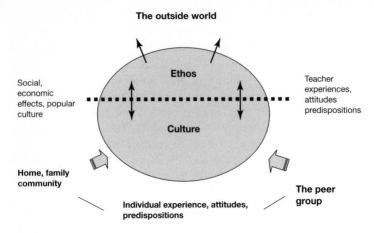

Figure 5.1 Ethos and culture

their fellow pupils and their teachers? Perceptions of unequal treatment and discrimination are a breeding ground of resentment and when left unaddressed can be powerfully undermining of attempts to build a learning culture. Carol Campbell and her colleagues (2001) propose four definitions of equality which offer a useful guide to evaluating inclusivity.

- formal equality of access and provision: concerned with explicit barriers to participation based, for example, on gender or 'ability' or disability;
- equality of circumstance: denial of opportunities because of someone's circumstances, poverty, parents, community factors;
- equity of participation, or treatment: informal aspects of school everyday life that allow some people to be treated less well than others;
- equity of outcome: the inequitable distribution of school benefits such as attainment outcomes.

As these four categories illustrate, equality and inequality may lie conspicuously on the surface or be deeply buried within the invisible logic of day-to-day practice. In investigating the deeper workings of discrimination within school cultures an important resource is the Gillborn and Mirza study for OFSTED published in 2000, *Inequality*.

Dalin and Rust (1996), two Norwegian educators, describe culture as operating on three levels corresponding broadly to the Freudian concepts of superego, ego and id. These three levels are:

The transrational: Values and norms operate at a 'metaphysical' level. There is a broad agreement on ideology or religion which binds people together in a common set of beliefs. There is a real sense of mission based on moral and ethical values and codes.

The rational: The rational culture is characterised by values and norms which are broadly accepted because they are ' conventional'. They abide by institutional rules, expectations and standards. They express daily routines, 'customs and ceremonies' of the school.

The sub-rational: Values and norms in the sub-rational derive from personal views, preferences, prejudices. They are grounded in emotion, intuition and subjective experience rather than on rational justification and express themselves more in the emotional voice than in the rational register.

QUESTION:

Thinking of your own school, or one you are familiar with, which of these three categories would it most closely resemble?

It may prove difficult to characterise a school as fitting easily into one of these three categories. In reality schools tend to be a more complex mix, at times operating more on a rational level, at other times more sub-rational. Individual departments, classrooms or groups of staff may be more rational than others, but it is likely that one of the three types will predominate at some times more than others. Just as in the human version of Freud's theory, the rational ego, the sub-rational id and the trans-rational superego are in constant struggle for supremacy at any given time, so may the organisational entity called a school.

In many of the attempts to evaluate and compare schools, nationally and internationally, they are treated as if they were rational structures. Studies of school effectiveness have often portrayed schools, intentionally or unintentionally, in terms of key functioning parts, as if schools could be made more effective by putting each of these in place: communication systems, discipline procedures, management strategies. Likewise, development planning has often been treated in a way which suggests that the future can be planned and that, with the blueprint in hand, people will dutifully follow its brief. Such a conception of development planning is described by Barbara MacGilchrist and her colleagues (1995) as 'rhetorical', that is trapped within a set of consecutive and logical words with no correlate in the reality of people's daily lives.

For evaluation to be meaningful, therefore, it has to transcend the assumptions of the rational, to take account of the rituals and conventions, and while giving them their valid place, striving to understand them more fully. Hampden-Turner and Fons Trompenaars (1993) wrote about 'a rationality of parts, an irrationality of the whole', meaning that it is only when we understand individual events within their wider context that we can usefully make useful judgements about the nature and quality of culture. This is not an argument for abandoning any attempt to 'measure' ethos or culture. Rather it is a counsel of wisdom to be careful as we go, and if we do focus on the singular atomistic detail of school life we must always come back to the big picture.

Ethos indicators

In the early 1990s a project was launched by the Scottish Education Department to identify indicators which would provide some quantifiable data on the school climate, complementing measures of pupil attainment. These were, eventually, given the title 'ethos indicators' and were to become an integral part of policy for school self-evaluation in Scotland. In recognition of the subjectivity of ethos, indicators were based on the perceptions of school life from the standpoints of teachers, parents and pupils and focused on relationships, the environment of learning, personal and professional satisfaction, the 'feel' of the school from the perspective of a visitor or as a daily participant in its on going life.

Ethos indicators were one element in a tripartite approach to school self-evaluation, described by the *Times Educational Supplement* (1993) as 'The threefold path to enlightenment'. The other two paths were through:

- A set of qualitative indicators based on criteria used by HMI in inspections of classrooms, departments and aspects of whole-school policy and practice;

• Relative ratings, which gave secondary schools formulae for calculating the differential effectiveness of subject departments.

Together these provided the pieces of jigsaw which, when complete, gave a picture of school as a corporate whole, coherent in its contra-dictions and internal anomalies. However, distribution of self-evaluation manuals to all schools by the Scottish Education Department did not guarantee commensurate enthusiasm on the part of schools, teachers or management. There were sceptics, doubtful that any good could come of it; there were outright opponents who saw it as an insidious under-mining of authority; there were the politicians who worked quietly to undermine its survival, and there were the 'precious' who saw ethos as too valuable a possession to be entrusted to pupils or parents.

It was acknowledged in retrospect as a mistake to try to infiltrate conservative school cultures through the cold sell of a manual dropping through the headteacher's letter box. It underestimated the passions that ethos indicators could arouse and the sensitivity to the feelings of those who saw themselves or their practices being exposed. Wise leadership, on the other hand, grasped the potential of these new tools as unlocking the closed doors to school improvement.

One simple form used to introduce ethos indicators to staff or to school boards is illustrated in Figure 5.2. This is a simple, subjective and impressionistic instrument, but what it does is provide a shallow-end entry into the issues, exploring the subjective domain, providing a locus for people to articulate and exchange their views and to embark on a more systematic approach to evidence. It raises the self-evaluation question 'How do we know?' and introduces the idea of a more systematic process of inquiry. It asks people to consider the questions 'How much of school ethos is in the eye of the beholder and how much of it can be described as an objective phenomenon?' and 'To what extent is it possible for a visiting inspector to categorise ethos with confidence as "good" or "excellent"?'

These twelve ethos indicators are, of course, only the beginning of the culture story, the tip of a large concealed mass beneath the waterline. They may hide undercurrents imperceptible to the member of the board but they do encourage deeper penetration and they ignite the desire for instruments, fine-tuned enough to plumb the greater depths.

Figure 5.3 provides another example of an ethos instrument containing within it deeper elements. It can be used with governors, management

Ethos Indicators	My view	Small group view	Board view
Pupil morale			
Teacher morale			
Teacher job satisfaction			
The physical environment			
The learning context			
Teacher-pupil relationships			
Discipline			
Equality and justice			
Extra-curricular activities			
School leadership			
Information to parents			
Parent-teacher consultation			

Figure 5.2 Ethos indicators – an introduction

teams, teachers, pupils, parents, or even a mixture of these groups as a starting point for dialogue, leading gradually deeper into more contested aspects of school life. The early items ask people to judge the school as warm/cold, welcoming/unwelcoming, colourful/drab, stimulating/boring – intuitive gauges of subjective feeling. Later items include risk-taking/avoids risks, pursues long-term goals/pursues short-term goals, avoids conflict/responds well to conflict, clear values/lack of clear values. These are, of course, much more difficult to answer and to 'know', but they place on the table things that really matter and provide the drivers of the warmth, the stimulation that people experience, or feel to be absent.

Improving school effectiveness

In 1995 the Scottish Office education department commissioned a study to evaluate current practices in evaluation of ethos and take us further

tidy	1	2	3	4	5	untidy
warm	1	2	3	4	5	cold
parent-friendly	1	2	3	4	5	parent-unfriendly
colourful	1	2	3	4	5	drab
authoritarian	1	2	3	4	5	democratic
comfortable	1	2	3	4	5	uncomfortable
orderly	1	2	3	4	5	disorderly
sensitive	1	2	3	4	5	insensitive
strict	1	2	3	4	5	easy-going
high-stress	1	2	3	4	5	low-stress
pessimistic	1	2	3	4	5	optimistic
tense	1	2	3	4	5	relaxed
helpful	1	2	3	4	5	unhelpful
competitive	1	2	3	4	5	uncompetitive
formal	1	2	3	4	5	informal
reactive	1	2	3	4	5	proactive
likes change	1	2	3	4	5	dislikes change
stimulating	1	2	3	4	5	boring
pupil-friendly	1	2	3	4	5	pupil-unfriendly
inflexible	1	2	3	4	5	flexible
clear values	1	2	3	4	5	no clear values
avoids conflict	1	2	3	4	5	responds well to conflict
adventurous	1	2	3	4	5	cautious
uses time well	1	2	3	4	5	time used badly
risk-taking	1	2	3	4	5	avoids risks
open to new ideas	1	2	3	4	5	sceptical of new ideas
idealistic	1	2	3	4	5	pragmatic
pursues long-term goals	1	2	3	4	5	pursues short term goals
looks to the past	1	2	3	4	5	looks to the future
....	1	2	3	4	5	....

Figure 5.3 Evaluating school ethos – the school as it is

down the road in developing insights into cultures of improvement. Figure 5.3 shows some of the items from an instrument used in that study (MacBeath and Mortimore, 2001). This instrument helped to explore layers of school culture deeper than ethos indicators because it tapped into the belief systems of staff. It revealed not only what people enjoyed or felt satisfied with but explored their expectations. It not only identified gaps between expectations and satisfaction, but revealed significant differences among different groups – pupils as against teachers, parents or school management – and within these groups. Not only did teachers, pupils and parents hold different perceptions and expectations, but within each of these groups there were also differences in what people wanted of their schools.

The quantitative data from the questionnaires also showed considerable variations between one school and the next, between different age groups and also within age groups. Some questions provided

This school now						The effective school				
1 2 3 4 5		Teachers as well as pupils learn in this school				1 2 3 4 5				
1 2 3 4 5		Teachers believe that all children in this school can be successful				1 2 3 4 5				
1 2 3 4 5		Teachers regularly discuss ways of improving pupils' learning				1 2 3 4 5				
1 2 3 4 5		Standards set for pupils are consistently upheld across the school				1 2 3 4 5				
1 2 3 4 5		Extra-curricular activities provide valuable opportunities for all pupils				1 2 3 4 5				
1 2 3 4 5		Teachers share similar beliefs and attitudes about effective teaching/learning				1 2 3 4 5				
1 2 3 4 5		Staff have a commitment to the whole school and not just their class or department				1 2 3 4 5				

This school now (left-hand side)
1 = strongly agree   4 = strongly disagree   5 = don't know

The effective school (right-hand side)
1 = crucial   2 = very important   3 = quite important   4 = not important   5 = DK

Figure 5.4 Teacher questionnaire (ISEP)

high levels of consensus while others provided a spread of responses; splits on any given issue proved to be as valuable and instructive as those for which there were high levels of agreement.

The inconsistency among pupil views sheds important light on the subjective nature of school experience and the differential impact which schools have on their pupils and on their teachers over time, not only year to year but week to week and day to day.

(p.80)

The value of an instrument such as this lies not in the objectification or quantification of the data that it provides, but in the power of leverage that it has as a 'tin opener' into the culture of the school itself. Its value is realised when it is used as an agenda for discussion, confronting the school with its own value system, its own currents and cross-currents of belief, its self-imposed inhibitions on its goals.

Ivan Illich (1971) describes an institution as something created to frustrate its own goals. Conventions, rituals and taken-for-granted practice can become so embedded that it is difficult to challenge them without some powerful levers such as the Improving School Effectiveness Project questionnaire provided. Questionnaires such as this are, of course, simply one tool that can be used to explore the culture of the school and need to be complemented by other approaches such as interviews, focus groups, shadowing and diaries. All of these are ways of making culture more amenable to examination.

The ISEP Project also used a device we called the change profile (Figure 5.5). Consisting of ten items about school learning, leadership and culture, its purpose was to engage a staff dialogue around issues of key concern in the school. Staff were asked to rate their school on a four-point scale from 'very like our school' to 'not at all like our school', first individually and then as a group. At the group stage they had to try to reach consensus by evidence-based advocacy. The headteacher and a critical friend also completed the profile independently so as to allow a triangulation of the data. As with the previous questionnaire example the disparity in perceptions provided the starting point for a deeper inquiry into the 'realities' of school life, revealing that the nature of experience depended significantly on the vantage point from which it was perceived.

1 = very like our school – 4 = not at all like our school

This is a learning school.	1	2	3	4
There are high expectations of pupil achievement.	1	2	3	4
There is ownership of change.	1	2	3	4
There are widely shared goals and values.	1	2	3	4
There is effective communication.	1	2	3	4
Pupil learning is a major focus of attention.	1	2	3	4
Leadership is effective.	1	2	3	4
There is real home-school partnership.	1	2	3	4
Relationships are based on respect for individuals.	1	2	3	4
Collaboration and partnership are a way of life.	1	2	3	4

Figure 5.5 The change profile

The SEP

The change profile provided the model for the self-evaluation profile (the SEP) used by the European Project in 101 schools (Figure 5.6). The model was adapted a) by the identification of twelve items that were common to the eighteen participating countries and b) by the involvement of parents, pupils and governors as well as teachers. Each of these four stakeholder groups filled out the SEP then sent two representatives each to a school evaluation group. This produced a group of eight people (nine including the head) who had then to try to reach a consensus on the basis of evidence while respecting differences and making an effort to learn from the various vantage points from which the school was being viewed.

The next stage was to agree on a specific area (or areas) for further in-depth inquiry, using finer-grained tools. So, for example forty-one of the 101 schools chose to explore the quality of learning and teaching over the course of the remaining year of the project.

In the brave new world we may devise instruments to measure with accuracy the hot and cool spots of the organisation similar to those now

	++	+	-	--	⬆	⬌	⬇

Outcomes

academic achievement							
personal and social development							
pupil destinations							

Process at classroom level

time for learning							
quality of learning and teaching							
support for learning difficulties							

Process at school level

school as a learning place							
school as a social place							
school as a professional place							

Environment

school and home							
school and community							
school and work							

Figure 5.6 The self-evaluation profile (SEP)

used in neurotechnology to measure human comfort, pleasure and depression. It is even possible with such technology to monitor people's emotional response to their context – a cerebral, scientific ethos indicator!

An approach developed by two Austrian researchers, Steiner-Löffler and Schratz (1996), provides a low-tech version of such an instrument, called photo-evaluation:

> Pupils can be given a still or video camera as an evaluation tool to explore the culture of their school as a learning organisation. The pupils' photographic or video images convey a different meaning from the one they might express verbally or in answer to a questionnaire. Moreover, pupils have to collaborate and work towards consensus building in selecting images worth photographing, so they form little communities of action researchers as they explore their daily school settings from a different perspective.
>
> (MacBeath, Schratz, Meuret, Jakobsen (2000), p. 152)

This approach may be seen as dealing more with aspects of ethos than culture since it focuses primarily on the physical aspects of the school, but it is also designed to be a tin opener, using the surface phenomena of school life to open up more fundamental issues of school structure and convention. It raises the issue of how we do things round here, but also how we might do things quite differently.

Photo-evaluation is primarily a tool for the schools' own self-evaluation and does not lend itself easily to data for reporting, accountability or for external inspection. However a school which has carried out a photo-evaluation can choose to present evidence to a visiting inspection team. It can use the photos to illustrate the underlying process, as a prompt to what has been learned and what has been put in place as a consequence. It may also be used to tell a story in words and pictures for a parent body or to the wider community.

A different kind of photo-evaluation was conducted by a primary school in Scotland, inviting in their critical friend to take a series of photographs over the course of one day then sifting through these to select the most telling and generative of them. It is described here by the headteacher at that time, Susan Ross.

> Here was visual evidence of relationships, pupil-pupil and teacher-pupil, giving us another focus to assess the ethos of the school and to deepen discussion on the school's main purposes and values. What did the photos say about the ethos we were trying to create? How could that ethos support and enhance pupils' ability to learn? A second parents' evening was held. With the questionnaire results as a backdrop to discussion parents were asked to work in small groups, listing all the things they thought made a 'good' school. They then had to select and agree on ten. Their next task was to look through the photographs and see if they could find evidence in Coalsnaughton School to match their criteria of a 'good' school.
>
> (Ross, 1995)

The learning school

Much has been written in recent years about learning organisations. It is only in the recent past, though, that the concept has been applied to schools and that we have begun to raise questions about how a school learns. An item in the ISEP questionnaire illustrates the extent to which this is still a foreign concept to many schools. The questionnaire contained the item 'Teachers as well as pupils learn in this school'. The overall response from eighty schools in the project was an agreement rate of 20% strongly agree, 28% agree (MacBeath and Mortimore, 2001).

QUESTIONS:

How would this item be responded to in your school?
How would you personally respond to it?

The question above refers to individuals seeing themselves as learners and behaving as learners. It would be unlikely to find a school in which everyone held to such a view, but that might not be the measure by which we judge a learning school. A school is more than the sum of its staff, and learning may reside within the structures and cultures of a school rather than in the individuals who inhabit those structures on a temporary basis. Learning, and learning to learn, lie deeper in 'the way we do things round here' and survive across generations and the transience of new heads, new staff, new pupils. Illustrative of how this needs to be modelled from the top, Cauther Tooley, head of Sarah Bonnell School in London describes herself on school notepaper and on her visiting card as 'Headlearner'. It is a public signal of the kind of school she wishes to create.

A learning school is one with a deep capacity to respond to situations intelligently. It has a reservoir of shared knowledge passed from one generation to the next. It has a repertoire of strategies and techniques to apply flexibly and appropriately to the issues at hand. It has an organisational memory and a distributed intelligence. Its litmus test is in the classroom, in the response to innovation and change by the ultimate gatekeeper:

> The class teacher is the ultimate gatekeeper in relation to change; perhaps the time has come to enable them to be at the forefront of change, rather than what seems evident at the present time, at the end of a long chain of responsibility passing.
>
> (Broadhead, 1995)

Schools in which staff feel disabled by a loss of control will find it impossible to give their attention to, and invest their enthusiasm in, organisational learning, and self-evaluation will remain at a surface level, a single loop of audit-plan-measure-implement.

Double-loop learning

The notion of the 'double loop' was invented by Chris Argyris (1993). It neatly encapsulates the process of self-evaluation and the character of the learning school. Single-loop learning obtains when audit, or self-evaluation, tools are used to give a picture of school culture at a given time. On the basis of this snapshot, steps are taken to address the issues raised. If attendance is low, initiatives are taken to raise attendance. If there is evidence of bullying, anti-bullying strategies are implemented. If standards are low, attainment targets are set. The OFSTED model of self-evaluation and inspection rests on such a view of school improvement.

The second loop interrupts the linear sequence. It involves standing back and taking a critical stance on the nature and meaning of the evidence. It entails a more holistic view on how things are interlinked within the deep structure and how they manifest themselves in the surface structure.

OFSTED, it is frequently said, has had a significant impact on schools, shaking them out of complacency and self-satisfaction. There is evidence to suggest that this is, in many cases, true (Lee, 2001). What is more at issue is whether it has provoked a more studied reflective approach. Or has it, as its critics charge, led to a more immediate tactical single-loop response?

QUESTION:

What is your opinion?

To qualify as 'double-loopers' schools need to able to reflect on and use their experiences of evaluation, and self-evaluation, with a shared desire to learn. It requires a desire to learn, not just about the collective experience but also from our own individual responses to that experience. What did it tell us about ourselves, individually and as a collective?

If the single-loop question is 'How good is our school?' the second-loop question is 'How good is self-evaluation in our school?' So, reviewing your school's learning from self-evaluation, or inspection, it may be examined at three levels:

- the technical level;
- the structural level;
- the cultural level.

At the technical level, a school might ask of itself: 'What did we learn about design, data, data-gathering, validity, the nature of "data", the context in which it is gathered, and about alternative ways in which we may gather data in the future?'

At the structural level, the questions are: 'What have we learned about the structures within which we gather and use data? What is there about those structures that facilitate and inhibit the gathering and use of data in a way that enhances our capacity to learn?'

At the cultural level, a school may ask: 'What did we learn about our responses? What are our defences? How habitual, and habit-forming are these? How deeply are these embedded in the way we do things round here?'

Can we honestly say we have a school culture which supports honest, self-critical reflection? How do we answer these following questions:

- How do we deal with dissent?
- How openly do we listen to viewpoints different from our own?
- How much do we trust the honesty and integrity of our colleagues?
- How much is our culture one of risk-taking?
- How much do we genuinely value learning from one another?

Binney and Williams (1997) suggest a large dose of humility:

> You can disempower somebody but you cannot empower them. They will really begin to change, taking initiatives, take risks, provide real feedback, learn from mistakes and accept responsibility for what they're doing when they feel sufficiently confident to do so and are provided with a clear framework. . . .Achieving this type of relationship is not easy. It requires much effort, openness and willingness to

learn – and some humility. It feels uncomfortable, particularly for leaders in organisations where this style is not the norm. It requires a high degree of self-belief and a willingness to try.

(p.69)

DISCUSSION:

You may like to consider the five questions suggested above in relation to your own school.

Learning disabilities

Without this self-critical perspective built in, schools may experience what Peter Senge (1990) calls organisational learning disabilities. Some commentators have described something similar which they describe as the 'competency trap' (Cousins, 1996). This is most characteristic of complacent, self-satisfied, often high-achieving, schools; schools blinded to ways in which they are disabled by their own self conceit. 'Nothing fails like success,' suggests Senge. We have all suffered the arrogance of successful individuals and have also had occasion to marvel at the modesty and learning disposition of others who are equally successful. So it is with organisational cultures. Their openness to learning is the hallmark of their social and psychological health and growth potential. It is through rigorous internal and external evaluation that schools become alive to their own disabling practices and develop a culture of learning.

In the NFER report for the Local Government Association *Evaluating School Self-evaluation* (Saunders 2001) the authors summarise the benefits to school culture and professional development under seven headings:

- School self-evaluation can help bring about a *change in the culture* of a school, helping to formalise and to extend existing processes of evaluating teachers and learning and data analysis.
- Teachers' *professional review* and *professional development* can benefit from schools' commitment to self-evaluation, particularly in schools where staff are encouraged to share expertise with colleagues and to take up training opportunities.

- For some headteachers, particularly those recently appointed, school self-evaluation has provided a mechanism with which to learn about their school and to *organise change*. In other words, evaluative processes, mechanisms and procedures may provide school senior managers with a framework (and 'levers') for the management of change.
- Schools can develop their *own agenda* for self-evaluation, enabling teachers to focus on aspects of the school that they identify as areas for improvement. Furthermore, the internal agenda set within schools can also help promote *ownership* among teachers of their self-evaluation activity.
- Schools can benefit from the support of a *critical friend*, whether an LEA adviser, consultant or colleague from another school. A critical friend who is external to the school can help teachers identify areas for development, meet the demands of a timetable for implementing and evaluating activities and can 'ask difficult questions'.
- *Parents, pupils and governors* can become involved in schools' self-evaluation work: to help set agendas for change and to benefit from evaluations of school policies and classroom practices.
- Self-evaluation packages and programmes, whether developed 'in house' by LEAs or 'bought in', can provide schools with a range of *tools* for implementing evaluation activities. These may take the form of questionnaires for parents and pupils, files for recording data, observation schedules and so on. 'Toolkits' for schools avoid the need for teachers to 'reinvent the wheel' and can facilitate sharing between schools using the same packages.

6 Benchmarking

Benchmarking is a term given to the process of measuring standards of actual performance against those achieved by others, identifying best practice, and taking appropriate steps to improve. Benchmarking may be against performance data, practice, behaviour, attitudes or perceptions. While benchmarking tends to be thought of in terms of 'hard' statistical data, governments rise and fall on the basis of people's perceptions, and policies in the media age are shaped powerfully by the benchmarking of public attitudes. Attitudes and expectations as benchmarks alongside performance data have, therefore, an important role to play.

Doing what comes naturally

If evaluation is simply a question of doing what comes naturally, then benchmarking falls into the same category. It is hardwired into our psyche to compare ourselves with some norm or standard – assessing what we are and what we feel we should be. As children develop, size and weight begin to matter more and more and become tortured issues as adolescence approaches, and they measure their physical attributes against cultural benchmarks provided for them by media, advertising, parents and peers.

Even before their child is born parents begin to worry about their 'normality'. They benchmark birth weight against a mean or norm and thereafter spend the next few years evaluating the stage at which their child smiles, crawls, walks, talks, reads, grows, performs well at school and surpasses, or falls short of, that high-stakes benchmark, IQ.

Benchmarking is so built into schooling that is it is difficult to imagine what schools would be like without it. The age structure of school assumes a level of knowledge and skills at each progressive stage. Curriculum and assessment are designed accordingly. SATs – standardised attainment tests – are standardised around age-related benchmarks. Pupils are measured, and measure themselves, against class or year averages, against aggregated SATs scores which assess the gap between where you are and where you could be, or should be, because a SAT score is never value-free. The first question a parent asks about a child's grade is not about its absolute, but its relative, value – in comparison to a classmate, a friend, the class as a whole. Fifty per cent has acquired a mythical status, virtually worldwide, as the dividing line between success and failure.

So what's new?

What is new is that governments have both formalised benchmarking and raised the stakes nationally and internationally. Although benchmarks have always been used by schools for both diagnostic and accountability purposes, the accountability purpose has been made much more trans-parent within the school, within the community and at a national level. The first school-by-school publication of examination attainment set in train a process that changed the currency of practice. The percentage attaining 5 A–C passes at GCSE became the key indicator of a school's effectiveness and improvement and passed indelibly into everyday language and thinking. With performance tables schools could compare themselves against national norms, local authority norms, or against other local schools or schools like themselves and, with this data to hand, could set targets for the next year and the year after that.

What's in it for schools?

Seen from the perspective of the classroom teacher, benchmarking has its dark side. As teachers and parents we struggle against the impossibility of convincing children to be their own people, not to follow the norm, not be angst-ridden because they are fatter, smaller, less well off, less clever or cleverer than their peers. We read of anxiety and stress in young children and are conscious of our own ambivalent attitudes to achieve-ment. We want our children and our pupils to do well, for all of them to be above average, but not at the expense of their happiness and fulfilment as human beings. We want them to 'be themselves'. Yet we cannot resist the need to be better both by our own standards and those of others. Teachers struggle from day to day with this delicate balance of pressure and support, being all you can be in your own terms and living up – or down – to the expectations of others. The challenging question is this:

QUESTION:

How can we use benchmarking in more formative, learner-friendly and teacher-friendly ways?

A step at a time

The first step in adopting benchmarking is, perhaps, as an individual, a group, a department or a school staff to clarify what we understand by benchmarking. What is the difference between a benchmark, a norm, an indicator and a target? While this question seems, on the face of it, quite straightforward, when we get down to answering it we usually find it is not so easy.

Figure 6.1 illustrates an activity that can be used fruitfully with a staff group to help clarify their thinking:

Working in groups of three to four and using the following grid write a short definition of what you understand by each of the three terms. Then in the box below give an example of each.

Benchmark	Indicator	Target

Figure 6.1 Benchmarks, indicators and targets – what do they mean?

Figure 6.2 illustrates the relationship of indicators to benchmarks and targets.

Benchmarks: targets and indicators

There is considerable confusion in this new vocabulary of indicators, benchmarks and targets, and the conceptual distinctions are not always clear. So how do we define these?

1. Benchmarks

A benchmark is not a target but an important piece of data to inform target-setting. It provides an individual, a class, a school or a school system with information against which to compare its own performance.

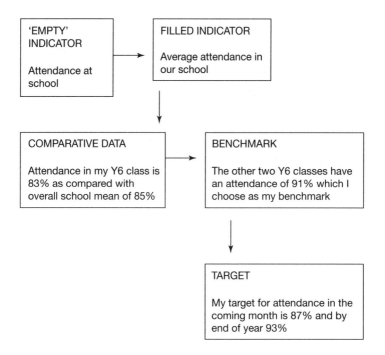

Figure 6.2 Indicators, benchmarks and targets – a flow chart

It shows standards achieved by members of the reference group, which might be other school subject departments, other schools locally, nationally or internationally. A benchmark is not simply an average of a norm. A school attendance average may be 85% overall, but the benchmark you choose for your class may be the level of the highest-achieving class: 91%. The norm, or average, is often taken as the benchmark, and in many cases it may be relevant, but these two things should not be confused. What you choose to compare yourself with – the best, the nearly best, or the average – will depend on where you are and how confident or ambitious you are.

DISCUSSION:

'The best is the enemy of the good.'

---

2. Targets

A target is something to aim for. It may be set completely without reference to anyone else or to any other institution. Many individuals set targets for themselves in their everyday life: to reduce from twenty to ten cigarettes a day, to walk for thirty minutes five days a week, to study two hours every evening, to get good grades. Teachers have, long before the discovery of targets by government ministers, set goals and targets for themselves and their classes. This was often accompanied by an informal kind of benchmarking against other classes, but not until this last decade has there been a formalised, mandatory approach to targets accompanied by penalties for failure. Targets are now routinely set by government bodies, by schools, by teachers and by pupils themselves. Benchmarks may prove useful as a reference point in deciding what target to set and sometimes the benchmark may itself provide the target to aim for. In the school where the average class attendance is 85% and the best-attending class achieves 91%, if in your class attendance is 83% you might choose 91% as a benchmark but set an immediate target of 87% with a goal for the future of 93%.

3. Indicators

Indicators are what we choose to underpin our quest for benchmarks and targets. Thus we might choose class size, teacher qualifications, pupil performance in science, or the percentage who say they enjoy school, as the indicator from which to derive our benchmark. The indicator is neutral, or 'empty' until we infill it with relevant data. When it is filled with data the indicator then provides information as to current performance or progress. This is usually accompanied by normative data which provides a comparative reference point, from which we may choose the best benchmark for our own needs and purposes. So our indicator may be 'average pupil attendance over the course of a school term' – an empty indicator until we find the data and then discover that it is 83%. This ceases to be value-free and takes on great significance as we compare this indicator across the school and with other schools from a similar socio-economic context.

Benchmarking attainment

Choosing what aspects of school life to benchmark says much about the values and priorities of the organisation. However, the freedom for schools to choose for themselves is constrained by government and local authority imperatives. The introduction of 'Key Stages' brought with it a high-stakes set of benchmarks, allowing a child's progress to be tracked throughout the course of their school life and a school to be

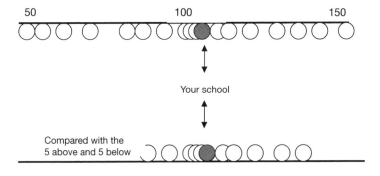

Figure 6.3 Comparing like with like

accountable for the value added at each stage. It brought with it an unprecedented transparency about the performance of an individual school and even of an individual teacher.

GCSE and A-level performance have long been standards by which schools and teachers benchmarked their own performance, but the annual publication of performance tables brought open, publicly comparative measures. Targets and benchmarks became mandated from a source outside the school. The inherent unfairness of what came to be known colloquially as 'league tables' was gradually acknowledged by policy-makers, and targets and benchmarking began to work on a basis closer to 'like with like'. In the last few years schools have become familiar with PANDAs, performance and assessment data supplied by OFSTED, enabling them to judge their own performance against national attainment data as well as against schools most like themselves. Schools are grouped in two ways: on the basis of free-meal entitlement (FME) and in relation to pupils' prior attainment. This allows two kinds of value-added monitoring, the prior attainment measure being the one generally regarded as the most useful.

Figure 6.4 is an example from a Scottish authority, East Renfrewshire, which provides schools with anonymised data from the ten schools most comparable to them in socio-economic terms – the five above and five below. In Figure 6.4, 100 represents a mean performance across all schools in the authority.

The local authority has its own benchmarks set against national standards and encourages schools to set targets with this as background

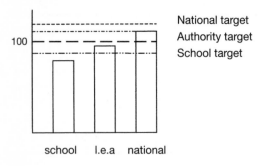

Figure 6.4 School, authority and national performance: percentage of pupils gaining 5 A–C passes

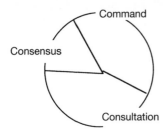

Figure 6.5 The balance of command, consultation and consensus

data as shown in Figure 6.5. The school may benchmark itself against the authority standard and set targets accordingly in consultation with authority advisers. The authority benchmarks itself against national standards in consultation with HMI.

Some examples of benchmarking used by schools

1. Boys and girls

To evaluate how well it was performing on the indicator of attainment by gender, a primary school analysed the overall percentage of boys and girls at the ages of seven, nine and eleven, attaining national targets for their stage in reading. The school then compared its own levels of attainment by gender with the relevant benchmark information for the attainment of boys and girls in reading as set out in national surveys. In light of this information the school found that boys were performing at about the level of the national benchmark but that girls were significantly underperforming. This prompted a new raised target for girls but, despite its relatively good performance by boys, the school set the same higher target for boys too.

2. Benchmarking motivation

A local authority undertook a random survey of students' views in Years 6 and 8 to examine changes in motivation after the transition from primary to secondary. Schools all pooled their findings so as to compare their own results with those of others. As well as being able to compare themselves against the norms for all schools, schools were able to identify schools similar to their own but achieving at a high standard of consistency between Years 6 and 8. These high-performing schools were chosen as the benchmark. (Some inspectorates carry out this kind of activity prior to an inspection and in this way are able to compare and contrast an individual school's standing with that of schools nationally. Staff then have the benefit of a national standard against which to compare their performance now and in the future.)

3. A mathematical equation

After a benchmarking exercise using national examination results, a mathematics department found that it was underperforming in relation to national averages. Comparing itself with mathematics departments in schools with similar free school meal figures it found it was performing considerably better than the norm; indeed it was the benchmark for other schools. It was not, however, satisfied with this and took as its benchmark the national average of all schools. This benchmark it adopted as its immediate target with a longer-term target of exceeding the national average.

Expectation shortfall

The following example is from the Improving School Effectiveness Project (MacBeath and Mortimore, 2001). It provides an example of benchmarking derived from teachers' attitudes to aspects of school life and culture. In this project teachers in eighty schools completed a fifty-four-item questionnaire from which these data are taken. Teachers were asked to respond to each of the items on the questionnaire in two ways: (1) assessing what they thought of the school now, and (2) saying what they thought would be important to make the school more effective.

So, as Table 6.1 shows, there is a gap between the real and the ideal. The ideal, an aggregate or average, of all teachers in the school might be treated as a target. That is, the school sets itself the aim of closing the gap between where they are now and where they want to be.

In doing so, however, schools wanted to know, for instance, what a 58% 'meant' for the item 'Pupils respect teachers in this school'. That is, they wanted to know how they compared to other schools. So, each

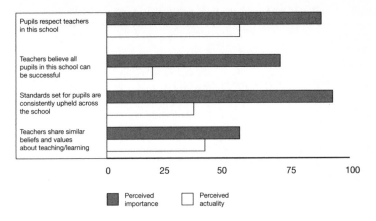

Table 6.1 Comparison of teachers' ratings of importance and actuality.

school was provided by the research team with an aggregate response from all other schools in the project so as to provide a norm to set against their own 'performance'. This did not provide them with a benchmark as many schools were, obviously, already performing above the norm. What they asked for were examples of schools which did significantly better than the norm in order to identify a better benchmark for themselves.

Table 6.2 shows the data from one secondary school compared with the mean of thirty-five secondary schools in the project. In this case the gap does not necessarily provide a target to be aimed at simply a point of reference. For example, on the item 'Teachers believe that all children in this school can be successful', 'your school' compares unfavourably with all schools but this norm still does not offer an acceptable benchmark. A more acceptable benchmark might be the figure on the right hand side of the table: the 75% who see it as a crucial underpinning belief system of an effective school.

Qualitative benchmarks

Most examples of targets, indicators and benchmarks are expressed in quantitative terms. As the data from the ISE Project illustrates, many aspects of school life, such as ethos, communication, and relationships

Table 6.2 Individual school data as compared with all schools in the project

AGREE			CRUCIAL	
Your school	All schools		**Your school**	All schools
58%	**48%**	Pupils respect teachers in this school	95%	**95%**
16%	**31%**	Teachers believe that all children in this school can be successful	70%	**75%**
58%	**58%**	Teachers regularly discuss ways of improving pupils learning	91%	**93%**
38%	**7%**	Teachers regularly observe each other in the classroom and give feedback	51%	**31%**
33%	**19%**	Standards set for pupils are consistently upheld across the school	96%	**93%**
35%	**22%**	Teachers share similar beliefs and attitudes about effective teaching/learning	55%	**60%**
57%	**48%**	Staff have a commitment to the whole school and not just their class or department	87%	**88%**

may be expressed in numerical terms. However, quantitative bench-marks tend to work on a linear scale, that is comparing higher and lower, better and worse. But benchmarks may also be expressed in other ways, as in the example in Figure 6.5. This indicates the balance of decisions made in a school in terms of command, consultation and consensus and may be arrived at by different routes. For example, it may the head's or the management team's judgement of the balance, and/or it may be calculated by a more studied monitoring and recording methodology among the whole staff. The end point is a reflection of the school as it 'is', but the benchmark might be taken as a balance of less command and greater consensus, or in quantitative terms: 10% command, 60% consul-tation, 30% consensus.

Benchmarks may work on a two-dimensional scale as in the well-known important/not important, urgent/not urgent matrix. This asks

Aspect	*Quantitative*	*Qualitative*
School performance resourcing ethos leadership		
Pupils attendance attainment attitudes behaviour		
Teachers performance professional development		
Parents information involvement		

Figure 6.6 Qualitative and quantitative measures

headteachers, governors or teachers (or, for that matter, pupils) to record their decisions about priorities – for example with regard to phone calls, letters, meetings with parents, marking, homework, leisure time, study for exams. The benchmark, as suggested by Steven Covey (1994a), should never be more than 2% urgent but not important.

At classroom level, a two-dimensional matrix such as that shown in Figure 3.2 (chapter 3) plots an aggregation of what thirty pupils in one class said about frequency of teaching methods and how effective they were from a pupil-learning point of view. For the teacher, the benchmarks might be taken as those activities rated as most effective.

So, benchmarks may be divided into quantitative and qualitative, and may apply across a whole range of school performances and processes. Figure 6.6 provides a framework for a teacher, staff working party or management team to think about the kinds of information and tools that might be used to benchmark different aspects of school life and learning.

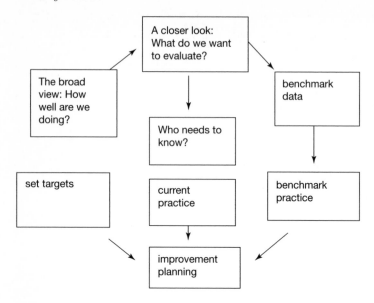

Figure 6.7 Benchmarking from broad view to closer look

From benchmarking to improvement: five steps

1. As in all moves to bring about improvement, the important thing is to get started. And getting started requires the culture to be right. In other words school staff at all levels need to be ready to respond openly to the question – 'How well we are doing?' and to seek answers with reference to other schools and other practice. This is always a task to be approached with caution, given a natural reluctance to be compared unfavourably and to admit that, as long-serving professionals, we still have lessons to learn from others perhaps less qualified and experienced than ourselves. Such willingness will, of course, depend to some extent on openness and support elsewhere in the system. Benchmarking is, after all, not just the responsibility of teachers and school management. It is also for advisers, inspectors and policy-makers, all of whom need to acknowledge the sensitivities and constraints of embarking on this exercise.

The way has to be prepared through discussion, training, informal exchange, emphasising improvement and potential rather than fault and blame. The selection of data and the evidence base need to discussed critically and sensitively with key stakeholders.

QUESTION:

Is there a readiness to get started?

- What is already in place?
- What is nearly in place?
- What do we still need to put in place?

---

2. Readiness for critical self-appraisal will be made easier if a range of voices and opinions have opportunities to be heard. Are the aspects of practice chosen those that really matter to the key stakeholders – their 'careabouts'? Knowing what they really care about, and consensus about aspects of school life that should be benchmarked, is part of the process of creating a receptive self-evaluating climate. Aspects chosen are those likely to have a direct bearing on students' learning and the effectiveness and efficiency of the organisation which supports that learning. So benchmarking comes to be seen as an integral part of the drive to school improvement and as an essential component of self-evaluation.

QUESTION:

What one or two aspects would you put in the 'really matters' folder?

---

3. Once you have selected the aspects that really matter, the next step is to take a broad view. This broad view will include the overall 'feel' of the school from different standpoints, and include different perceptions of how well the school is doing in this or that aspect. If school, regional or national benchmarks already exist, these may provide a starting point.

The broad view is useful in identifying a few selected areas of focus and priorities for action. Being selective enables you to get things moving quickly with a minimum of extra effort and can help to penetrate the mystique which often surrounds evaluation. In the early days it is particularly helpful to benchmark against schools with similar backgrounds to your own as this helps to give a sense of fairness to the practice – a comparison of like with like which can serve to disarm the critics and the cynics.

QUESTION:

How might you make use of the broad view approach in your school or school system?

4. Having benchmarked your performance using the broad view, the next step is to take a closer look at your key priorities – those aspects where you are falling short of your chosen benchmarks and where you feel there is scope for improvement. Your closer look should aim to explain the reasons for your underperformance in relation to the chosen benchmark and begin the process of identifying what specific aspects of practice need to be addressed. This is where self-delusion or self-protection has to give way to rigour.

We have, in this book, concentrated on three broad areas of evaluation: learning and teaching, ethos and culture, management and leadership. Whatever focus you choose it is likely to fall within one of these three broad areas.

QUESTION:

Are the core aspects the right ones? Would you start with them?

5. Having examined the aspects that matter to you in relation to school, regional and/or national benchmarks, you are now in a position to decide how you can translate any lessons learned into your own practice. This is the 'planning for improvement' stage – the 'What are we going to do now?' question. This may require returning to the school development

plan to take account of the aspects which you wish to incorporate as part of your improvement plan. It is here that target-setting comes into its own. It is the concrete response to what, as a school, you are setting out to achieve over say the next six months or a year. This is the 'What must we do to make it happen?'

Your closer look at the core aspects is likely to throw up the need for targets which focus on students' performance. Sample targets might include:

- To increase the attendance rate of students in Year 9 to the level of the local authority benchmark within two years;
- To increase attendance at study support by 20% next year and by 30% the following year;
- To improve the performance of pupils at Key Stage 2 in line with national averages;
- To increase the proportion of pupils gaining GCSEs at A–C by 5 per cent in the coming year.

QUESTION:

How would you ensure that aspects such as pupils' attitudes and values, and personal development and behaviour are not lost in the desire to be SMART?
(Specific, Measurable, Attainable, Realistic, Time-Contained)

You are now well into the *implementation* and finally the *monitoring and review* stages of benchmarking for school improvement.

QUESTION:

Interaction: How would you go about this?

Ten basics of benchmarking

1. Understand what you are trying to do and why, and be clear about how you will use the information.
2. Make sure the culture is ready and take one step at a time – the broad view followed by the closer look.
3. Start by analysing your current performance: 'How well are we doing?'
4. Choose the things that are important to benchmark, not just those for which data are readily available.
5. Compare your performance with those of similar schools: 'How well should we be doing?'
6. Be open and share what you are doing with key stakeholders: teachers, parents, students.
7. Set yourself clear and measurable targets: 'What more can we aim to achieve?'
8. Revise your development plan to highlight action to achieve the targets – 'What must we do to make it happen?'
9. Take determined action to improve and evaluate success.
10. Engage in dialogue which treats data open-mindedly and with caution and listens to the dissident voices.

Above all, promote benchmarking as an integral part of your culture of 'evaluating and improving the effectiveness of your organisation to raise pupils' achievements'.

QUESTION:

How would you in your school go about ensuring that the ten basics of benchmarking are carried through?

7 Preparing for inspection

The art of connoisseurship – the ability to see what is there as well as what isn't there. – Elliot Eisner

A mature system of evaluation is one in which self-evaluation is robust and self-confident, welcoming of the external inspector at any time because the school has nothing to hide and much to show off about. So we argued in chapters 1 and 2 of this book.

What percentage of schools in any system would feel this way? Perhaps a relatively small minority. More typical at present is apprehension at the arrival of the brown envelope, signalling a period of intense preparation, meetings, rehearsal, extra investment of time and energy, extra levels of stress. Even in the best prepared of schools there is a desire to present its best face to the outside world, just as any household would make special preparations before receiving a visitor.

There can be few schools which still harbour the notion that 'it won't happen to me', but there are some who believe it will not happen 'yet' and so, when faced with the unannounced visit, or the intimation of a future visit, respond with panic. HMI and OFSTED inspectorates offer similar 'words of counsel' which may be paraphrased as:

1. Recognise it will happen sometime.
2. Assume it can happen tomorrow.
3. Consider how ready the school would be.
4. Identify the evidential basis for that judgement: 'What and how do we know?'

5.   Review self-evaluation: 'How embedded is self-evaluation across the school?'
6.   Reflect on priorities: 'Do we evaluate the aspects that really matter?'
7.   Test the development plan: 'Is it meaningful to parents and pupils?'
8.   Find out what happens before, during and after an inspection – and share with staff.
9.   Be prepared: have your set of school documents readily available.

School leaders who have not observed such counsel find themselves engaged in a camouflage exercise, 'planting the daffodils and burying the bodies', as one London headteacher put it. Their failure to 'be prepared' puts extra stress on the teachers who are at the forefront of an inspection. This can be an intense, time-consuming and fraught activity, all of these in direct proportion to the integrity of self-evaluation in the school's daily life.

The seven deadly sins of pre-inspection

The term 'inspection' does conjure up images of army sergeants, high-sheen boots, immaculate beds and painting the coal white. Perhaps this popular image of inspection is what encourages schools to emulate army practice in preparation for an OFSTED visit. But while it is natural for schools to wish to present their best face to their eminent visitors it can be counterproductive to try to fool them with cosmetic change. The following are some commonly committed 'sins' of pre-inspection, many of which are sure to find you out.

1. A sudden splash of colour

Teachers and headteachers understand that inspectors like to see good use being made of wall space – in reception areas and corridor areas as well as in classrooms. Many a dark outbuilding or annex has been brought alive through judicious use of colour, visual images and examples of pupils' achievements. There are many schools where display is an integral part of the development plan and subtly exploited as a means to promote learning, to encourage a pride in the place, to project a positive and bright image, to evoke a response from pupils and teachers (and visitors) and to celebrate success. In such schools, the inspector doesn't have to dig deep to uncover the connections with what is happening in the classroom: a philosophy which brings together the activities of the whole school, uniting staff and pupils.

In sharp contrast is the situation where schools, just before the inspection, cover the walls with materials of all kinds – its main purpose being impression management. Few inspectors are, in fact, taken in by a splash of colour. Most can spot such 'quick fixes' without great effort and tend to see it as an affront to their professionalism. Such cosmetic cover-ups tend to be quickly exposed.

2. *The virtual classroom*

The same principle applies in the classroom. Bare classroom walls can suddenly be transformed prior to the inspector's visit. Pupils' work suddenly emerges from its resting place in the cupboard and the class enter into a collusion with the teacher to produce a display for the occasion. We know of one art teacher who, in the week prior to an OFSTED inspection, borrowed pupils' work from a colleague in a neighbouring school.

It often takes little to expose the fraud. At the end of a lesson on the castles of Scotland, a pupil was asked by the teacher to name a castle fitting the description she had just given. Seeing he was stuck, the teacher, a little agitated by the presence of the 'man in a suit', drew the boy's attention to the charts with the words 'It's all there on the wall. Don't you *see*?' The boy, with no malice intended, responded: 'This is the first time I've seen these pictures, miss.' The sad thing about this story is that the quality of the lesson was such that the teacher had no need to impress the inspector and her duplicity simply served to weaken her impact.

3. *The new teaching experience*

Sometimes teachers will introduce a new teaching approach and try to pass it off as a standard part of their repertoire. This all too often takes the form of a machine that won't work, a lost image, a wobbly picture, distorted sound, the wrong video being shown. All of these present transparent evidence that the teacher has made little or no use of videos in the past.

One teacher, learning that a particular inspector was keen on brainstorming, organised not one but several lessons based on this 'new' approach in the hope that the inspector would call at the right moment. The inspector did and witnessed a chaotic lesson in which no one, including the teacher, quite knew what was happening. Several pupils told the inspector afterwards that they were looking forward to the end of the inspection and 'all this stupid brainstorming'. The moral: teachers should stick to what they know and do best. An inspection is not the time to surprise pupils, who can be astute observers of the incongruent and disingenuous.

4. *It was all right at rehearsal*

It would be unnatural for teachers not to prepare their class for the visit of an inspector. How the event is portrayed, its focus and purpose, may be honest, benevolently misleading, or blatantly dishonest. In our own experience as pupils we tended to believe our teachers when they told us that inspectors would be coming to observe us, sometimes with dire threats about the consequences of misbehaviour. Pupils today are less likely to be fooled but they will usually be willing to enter into a pact with their teachers against the outsider. One of the techniques, now enshrined in mythology, is the instruction to the class: 'If you know the right answer to the question put up your right hand. If you don't know the answer put up your left hand.'

One teacher who admitted to this sleight of hand described how it had been exposed, innocently she thought, by a pupil who put up his right hand to ask: 'Sorry, miss, could you tell us again which hand it was to put up?'

5. *The overnight policy paper*

It is headteachers, more often than teachers, whose judgement goes awry at the prospect of an inspection. Development plans emerge, to even the most unpractised eye, recently composed in haste. There are numerous cases of heads working weekends, rewriting policy papers or writing them for the first time. Experienced professionals have been trained to spot the 'fresh paint' and discussion with staff quickly confirms the depth or shallowness of the veneer. When notice is given of a forthcoming inspection it is too late to attempt to fill and paint over the cracks and, in the event, highly counterproductive. The evidence that inspectors seek is the depth and breadth of commitment of a staff to the school's mission and priorities. The stronger the contrast between what is on paper and what happens in practice the harder the judgement that an inspection team will make. Inspections are essentially concerned not with the present but with the past and the future: what has been done over time, what actions have been taken, with priorities turned to achievements, and clear visions for their realisation in the future.

6. *The backdated memo*

It is not unknown for some *post hoc* activity to take place in the weeks running up to the inspectors' call. The complete lack of correspondence on file has prompted the odd school to rectify the situation with new additions to the file or the simple predating of minutes, memos or letters. This is a dangerous game as it doesn't take a detective like Columbo to follow an audit trail and ask a few probing questions. While in some instances the uncovering of such deliberate fraud may be a relative peccadillo, in some instances it may be construed as a sacking offence, especially where it involves the complicity of support staff.

7. *Singing from the same hymn sheet*

It is natural perhaps for senior management to wish to convey the impression of a united staff, sharing common beliefs and telling the same story. This is sometimes carefully rehearsed. Like evidence for the defence, accounts are aligned in detail. But as with witnesses whose stories cohere too easily, the more similar the testimony the less believable it is. Every organisation is characterised by differences in perspective, healthy disagreement and debate. Experienced inspectors know this.

We know of one case where for the follow-up to an inspection, the headteacher issued the staff with a list of the kind of questions which he anticipated would be pursued by the inspectors. While that may have been no more than a sensible course of action, he also provided the answers and, by inference, staff's agreement to the claims made on progress on 'action points' from the original report. The intention was to ensure that all staff 'sang from the same hymn sheet'. The plan became unstuck before the end of morning break when a teacher passed the 'crib sheet' to the lead inspector: an action which in itself spoke volumes about the real cohesiveness of the staff. The school failed the inspection. An ethos of working together for improvement through self-evaluation had still to take root.

Sugar-coating

These seven sins are reflected in a recent study by a Cambridgeshire teacher (Dannaway, 2001). Summarising her students' views of the inspectors' visit, she reported five key changes in the school.

- The relative *change in attitude* of staff and students: 'Everyone is telling us what to say and how to act. What's this – a dictatorship? Are we expecting Stalin or Hitler next week?'
- *Special lessons* being put on for show for the inspectors. Students discussed at great length how their motivation changed when the normal style of teaching was taken over by more challenging lessons and a general disruption to their routine.
- The *look of the school*, which they felt became more polished and suitable for visitors at any time of the day; staff bemoaning the fact they had put on the show constantly, ever ready for an inspector's visit.
- *Trouble was well hidden* during OFSTED week. 'Trouble students' were sent away to an outdoor pursuits centre to partake in a week-long alternative education programme.
- The *changing atmosphere* in the school was described as a rising continuum of stress. Students noted how stress and anxiety permeated the atmosphere of their school leading up to the inspection, as did a feeling of fear and expectation during 'the visit' itself. This was dispelled in the week after OFSTED when, 'everything returned to normal'.

When it was suggested that the students write their experiences for the local newspaper their response was 'Should we sugar coat it, miss?' With some further counsel from the headteacher the pupils' comments, largely favourable but mildly critical, appeared under the headline 'OFSTED and us – no problem'. Dannaway concludes:

> At times, as I strain to remember some of the heated atmosphere that surrounded our discussions during my research sessions, I do think

about the fickle nature of youth. When I look at the newspaper and read the students' words I admire their courage and their naivety. In the end what was important to them was their school, their name, their words and their faces in a well read local paper printed clearly for all to read. If I learnt something from this experience it's that kids don't *sugar-coat the truth* because somewhere along the way they decide what is public and what is private.

(Unpublished paper)

Cheating?

While all of these may be seen as examples of 'cheating', some ploys and subterfuges are more excusable than others. The dishonesty of the head who asks staff to deny or cover up a problem is an indicator of a deeper-seated malaise in the culture and is likely to invite an inside informer to spill the beans. From time to time inspectors are told, usually in a whisper, by a teacher, a neighbouring head or education authority official that 'you got it wrong in that school'. It may be someone with a grudge against the school or someone whose own inspection report was felt to be unfairly negative.

'Wrong' in this context typically means that the report was too generous to the headteacher and/or the school overall. Staff who have suffered under a glib head who appears to have snowed the inspection team can harbour resentment that incompetence and dissimulation were not exposed. Heads who have lazy or incompetent teachers can also point inspectors in their direction in order to have a voice of authority on their side.

Whatever the judgement, 'cheating' is more likely to weaken rather than strengthen the culture of the school. In contrast, when self-evaluation is 'owned' by the school and staff can stand with confidence behind their findings a school can prepare for an inspection with optimism and integrity.

Briefing

An aspect of an accountability culture is for inspectorates to be subject to a code of practice. They can be expected to provide a briefing on the process of inspection, outlining what will happen from the moment of first contact with the school. Schools will be made aware, or reminded, of the criteria against which they will be assessed. Briefings from the four United Kingdom inspectorates would normally be expected to include the following:

- Purpose of the inspection;
- Key features of the inspection (e.g. whole-school inspection, sample of subjects, care and welfare);
- The inspection process (e.g. timetable, one or more phases, feedback to staff, interviews);
- The format of the report;
- Publication of the report (including arrangements for discussion of the draft);
- Follow-up to the report (e.g. the school's part, the inspectorate's part);
- Briefing should be geared to the needs of the key stakeholders, including teachers, headteachers, parents and pupils, boards of governors or school boards.

Information overload

Increasingly, inspectorates are cutting back on the amount of information they request in advance of an inspection. The result is a new indicator of success for the inspector: how good are schools at getting across their story in a concise number of pages. The Modernising Government Unit uses the same approach for its Charter Mark applications – twelve pages being the limit. Experience shows that, despite good advice to keep it short, some headteachers continue to add more and more information beyond what is asked for. The standard joke that 'you need a barrow to deliver all the stuff to the inspectors' is no laughing matter for staff as the writing and gathering of material in excess of what is asked for simply adds to the school stress factor and hampers effective preparation in the run-in to an inspection. Such behaviour also raises questions about the school's abilities to prioritise and summarise key messages. Nor is it a welcome prospect for inspectors to plough their way through volumes of material. They prefer, at the time of inspection, to ask for additional illustrative material to illuminate issues as they arise.

Knowing what inspections are about – the headteacher's job

Despite all the publicity, the stories of stress and the generally high profile of inspections, there are still headteachers who are unaware of what happens before, during and after an inspection. This is unforgivable in light of evidence of how stressful inspections can be for teachers. The evidence also suggests that the more teachers know about what is going to happen during an inspection the more relaxed they become. The management team that is in command of the facts and who, at the right moment, shares its knowledge with the staff (and pupils and parents) is most likely to have a school which is ready to take on the challenge of an external inspection.

How do we compare? – what will an inspection report say about us?

Well in advance of the actual event, headteachers should obtain copies of published reports to get a feeling for their tone and style, and for the nature and type of comment made. An effective management team will begin to think about how the school and its own self-evaluation will stand up to an inspection. Inspectorates have suggested that schools should be asking themselves questions such as:

- How do we compare?
- What would appear under 'key strengths' and 'main points for action' when we are inspected and reported upon?
- Do our practices and policies match, exceed or fall below the practices illustrated in the reports?
- What would HMI say about us?

What is required of schools in advance of an inspection?

The notification of inspection letter starts the gathering of essential information from the school. While the procedures vary from country to country, there is now a fairly consistent approach to inspection, with more similarities than differences.

Failure to prepare ahead can result in the situation well known to us where the head and the school are scrambling around to draw together the material and the resultant crisis and uncertainty is the worst possible preparation for the impending inspection.

The most recent advice from OFSTED and HMI in Scotland sets out their requirements in a clear and unambiguous manner. It makes sense for schools to have the following information to hand:

- Basic information about the school roll and attendance;
- Details of staffing;
- Information about the curriculum structure and timetabling;
- Aims and policies;
- A school handbook;
- A school plan and details of progress made in meeting the priorities in previous plans;
- Analysis of pupils' attainment, details of pupil progress made towards meeting the school's agreed targets, usually supplied by OFSTED and HMI.

In England, schools have their PANDAs: elaborate performance and assessment data sometimes running to fifty pages. Clearly a working knowledge and intelligent use of PANDAs is something inspectors will want to see.

Another feature of the OFSTED approach is the 'headteacher's statement', which invites the head to comment on:

- the characteristics of the school;
- monitoring and evaluation process;
- the overall effectiveness of the school;
- improvement since last inspection;
- priorities for development;
- pupils' personal development;
- teaching and learning;
- what the school offers its pupils;
- equality of opportunity;
- guidance and support.

What happens during and after an inspection?

While the details may vary from inspectorate to inspectorate, most use a range of methods which include focus on:

- Pupils' performance in classwork and examinations;
- Class visits to consider the overall quality of learning and teaching and ethos;
- Key features of attainment across the school;
- Interviews with groups of pupils and staff;
- Interviews with, where appropriate, parents, boards of governors or school boards;
- Provision for the care and welfare of pupils, including child protection policies and practices;
- Accommodation, including social areas and toilets;
- School documents and records (for example, disciplinary, attendance and accident records; minutes of main school committees/boards);
- Key aspects of leadership and management, with a particular focus on the school development plan, and the school's procedures for self-evaluation and improving its effectiveness, including, in particular, the action being taken to raise pupils' levels of attainment.

Self-evaluating schools are producing their own report outlining how good their school is and what it is doing to improve further: a standards and quality account to their pupils, parents and the school community. The advice here is to get started, to be open in your evaluations and beware of self-delusion – concealing the real messages is simply cheating yourself and your pupils. Getting started sets an improvement agenda for the benefit of your pupils and will bring praise from the external evaluator. If you are not into self-evaluation, then you are in for a rather unpleasant shock when 'an inspector calls'.

The devils (and the angels) are in the detail

It is often the small, and apparently insignificant, details that say much about the ethos of a school. The following incident that took place in the reception area of a London primary school took less than a minute but left a strong impression with the visitor (in this case not an inspector).

While attending to the visitor the teacher noticed a small child looking around anxiously. Excusing herself for a moment, the teacher went over and bent down to speak to the boy. She listened patiently for about half a minute while he struggled to tell his story. With a smile and reassuring hand on his shoulder she guided him to the office and made sure he was attended to. She returned and apologised to the visitor for the interruption.

The priority given to the needs of the child, the transparent concern and skill of the teacher were a significant indicator of the school's culture and, to the practised eye, not merely a demonstration intended to impress. Indeed, a self important visitor might have taken offence.

Even more trivial in a sense is the following tale of the broken umbrella. It carries carry within it a moral for the HMIs involved.

The case of the broken umbrella!

Effective headteachers know that the office manager or secretary is the front line, the creator of 'good impressions'. An inspector whose umbrella had been rendered more or less useless by the force of the wind was welcomed by an ever-alert secretary, who told him to 'forget about the umbrella', reassuring him with the promise 'I'll bring forward the coffee for your meeting'. At the end of the visit, he was handed back his umbrella – now as good as new. The headteacher smiled, saying of the secretary, 'She is a fixer'. She was widely acknowledged as someone with a central role in establishing and maintaining the school's welcoming ethos. Parents tell researchers and inspectors that being made welcome on arrival is probably the key to a good meeting and generating a feel-good factor. Self-evaluating schools, like the one in our example, heed this advice and act on it.

This is why office staff are key players in self-evaluation and need to be included in preparation for inspections. An inspector tells the story that while waiting to meet with parents, he talked to office staff about photographs of staff on the reception area wall. The conversation moved naturally into a discussion of staff who had made a special contribution to the school. The office staff were quick to identify three particularly effective departmental heads and 'the number one teacher' in the school. The basis for their decisions emerged with comments like 'You should see the quality of his teaching notes, so clear'; 'The pupils just love to be in her class, you can see it in their faces'; 'he is the first to step forward when something needs to be done'; and 'Mr X just bounces into school.'

LOOKING IN THE DUSTBIN – A LESSON FROM THE COMMERCIAL WORLD

With 105 stores, and three billion poundsworth of sales, Morrison's is a medium-sized, value-for-money chain in the north of England and Scotland. In a recent interview in the *Daily Telegraph*, Sir Ken Morrison was asked to explain his success in competing with the 'big boys' in retailing. In response he asks himself 'What's the most important place I look when I go round a store? The dustbin. That's where all the grief ends up, isn't it? It's a good guide to how a store is run. You don't go and see if the front door's been polished, do you?'

Drawing on the dustbin analogy, the following is a useful self-evaluation exercise which we have used with schools:

1. Staff work in pairs at a table of eight. On the table is a sheet of flip-chart paper divided into four with a circle left blank in the middle (see Figure 7.1).
2. Each pair jot down in their own quadrant a number of things that might be found in the school dustbin: for example, things they would not wish to show the visitor or an inspector.
3. These are then shared in the group of eight and agreement is reached on two or three common items that need to be removed from the dustbin and made visible.
4. Each table then pin their chart on the wall so that a full discussion can take place as teachers wander around and compare ideas.
5. From the ideas and the discussions, a school can produce its own 'ethos indicators' or indicators of hidden things that matter.

An item that appears frequently on these lists is school toilets. Questions, or indicators, that arise from discussion include:

1. Are the pupils' toilets clean, accessible and safe for pupils, both the younger and the older ones?
2. Are the toilets open throughout the school day, and monitored and checked by the staff on a regular basis?
3. Is there a regular supply of basics: toilet paper, clean towels?

In St Modan's High School, Stirling, pupils have been given ownership of the toilets, and bright colours, mirrors, pictures and flowers have transformed the image. The importance a school gives to its toilets tells the inspector a lot about the ethos of the place.

What do *you* think? What matters in *your* school?

The inspector's art

Inspection has been criticised by some researchers as 'unscientific', failing the reliability and objectivity test. Inspectors could not, and would not wish to, defend what they do on scientific grounds. The ground on which they would rest their case is connoisseurship, described by Eliot Eisner (1991) as the 'ability to see what counts'. Comparing novices and experts, he says: 'The expert knows what to neglect. Knowing what to neglect means having a sense for the significant and having a framework which makes the search for the significant efficient' (p.34).

He describes the complementary qualities of schema and sensibility. Schema is the frame, the way of seeing the whole picture. Sensibility alerts the observer to the nuanced qualities in the situation. Together scheme and sensibility, the 'subtleties of the social', are made meaningful.

Schools and classrooms are subtle and complex places. It requires a high degree of social and emotional intelligence to see beyond their superficial features. It is only recently that science has begun to recognise that there is such a thing as intuition, an ability to 'read' social situations, to see what isn't visible. This is not to argue that inspectors or other experienced observers can take the high ground. Observations and interpretations can be wrong. So they must be open to challenge and discussion. But this is also the mark of connoisseurship: the conviction not only to make judgements but the confidence to listen to alternative interpretations.

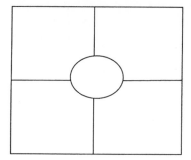

Figure 7.1 The 'table mat' exercise

A smile on the face of the teacher

The connoisseur inspector is alert to signals from staff and asks, 'What do the faces tell us?' Casually but with meaning, inspectors observe teachers as they go about their daily business, coming along corridors, entering and leaving classrooms. They pick up exchanges between teachers and pupils. Is the message one which says 'The teachers like coming through the school door every day?' Are they are happy in the classroom? Is there a 'real smile' culture? These indicators do no more than complement other sources of judgement on ethos and culture, but they are often more perceptible to the outsider than to the insider who lives with the school day in and day out. It is salutary for staff to stand back, to put themselves in the position of the outsider – what the Icelander calls 'the visitor's side-eye view'. In Csikszentmihalyi's books *Flow* (1990) and *Creativity* (1996), he urges us to 'write down each day what surprised you and how you surprised others'. The table mat exercise (Figure 7.1) is designed for a group of four. Each member writes in their quadrant two or three things they have learned or been surprised by. They then agree on two or three common items to write in the central circle.

Sending a message to parents

The 'enlightened eye', as Eisner calls it, applies with equal force to the fresh, visitor's eye, reading of school documentation. It looks with schema and sensibility at the style and tone of letters, reports and information leaflets, asking questions such as 'Is this letter likely to evoke a response from parents? Do the leaflets convey a sense of audience? Is the communication personal or impersonal, inviting or uninviting?' Answers to these questions provide further small pieces in the impressionistic evidential jigsaw that inspectors put together.

The ability to see what is there as well as what isn't there is the art of connoisseurship. It is not a unique gift of inspectors. It is something that can be learned by teachers and headteachers, and by pupils too. It is a precondition of effective school self-evaluation.

8 Evaluating leadership

'The clearest message from school effectiveness research' says John Gray (1988), is the importance of leadership. Sammons, Hillman and Mortimore (1994) concur: 'Almost every single study of school effectiveness research has shown both primary and secondary leadership to be a key factor' (p.78).

Scottish HMI put it this way: 'The leadership qualities of headteachers and the manner in which they fulfil their management responsibilities are key factors in determining the effectiveness of schools' (2000, p. 2). The DFEE White Paper *Excellence in Schools*, (2001) raises the stakes even further with the claim: 'The quality of the head often makes the difference between success or failure of a school' (p. 8). With this as an underpinning, a succession of government initiatives in the last half-decade have put management and leadership centre stage in policy development.

Studies of schools and their effects have given impetus to this emphasis on leadership and to the worldwide quest for the essential attributes or competencies of leaders. The driving questions are: 'What makes good leaders?', 'How are good leaders made?', 'Can leadership be learned or is it a gift?' In search of the answers studies have taken different forms and have been grounded in different assumptions. We may describe different types of studies of leadership as having four main dimensions:

- Quantitative and qualitative;
- Inductive and deductive;
- Subjective and objective;
- Behaviourist and constructivist.

Quantitative and qualitative

Quantitative approaches are those which draw on large samples, whether of headteachers, teachers, pupils or other parties, with the aim of producing numerical data robust enough to draw some general conclusions about the characteristics or effects of leadership. Falling within this broad category are studies of different kinds. They include questionnaires, distributed to large samples, typically asking respondents to agree or disagree with a series of propositions about leadership and management. There are correlational studies which set out to find relationships between certain kinds of schools and certain kinds of school leaders, including what are known as 'direct effect' studies. These try to find a direct relationship between what leaders do and what pupils achieve. So, for example, leadership effectiveness would be demonstrated by finding a direct relationship between measured pupil outcomes and measures of the leader's performance.

The tight linking of pupil and headteacher performance has had a seductive appeal to policy-makers who have seen in this a way of holding school leaders to account. For example, in the United States performance-based accountability has recently been given a new lease of life under the Bush administration. Some states had already been employing rewards-and-sanctions policies for school principals. In New York City schools, for example, principals can receive up to $15,000 in bonuses for major test score gains by their pupils.

Less appealing to impatient policy-makers are 'mediated effects' studies. These assume a less direct route, correlating leadership characteristics with process measures such as teacher morale, job satisfaction or professional development. Strong correlations here, it is assumed, will have a direct bearing on pupil outcomes: the happier and more committed the teacher the better her pupils will perform. It may simply involve waiting a little longer to test the premise.

Other quantitative methods include meta-level studies – studies of studies – which set out to find across a range of investigations a common core of consensus on what constitutes effective leadership. The Sammons, Hillman and Mortimore study quoted above reached its conclusion on the basis of an extensive international survey of the field.

Qualitative approaches, too, cover a sizeable terrain. These generally look for depth rather than breadth. They typically take the form of interviews, perhaps with heads or management teams, or with teachers, parents and pupils. They may, like quantitative studies, aim to arrive at common features of leadership which apply across contexts and cultures. With a large enough sample, qualitative data may be turned into quantitative measures, with the help of sophisticated software, searching through interview transcripts for common themes. Other methods of collecting qualitative data include diaries and logs, observational studies, case studies, biographies and other written narratives. Using drawings in which leaders depicted themselves and the context of their work proved to be a powerful qualitative medium in one international study (MacBeath, 1998). It not only helped to overcome the barriers of language but provided a starting point for deeper digging into attitudes, belief systems and conceptions of leadership (Figure 8.1 is an example of a drawing done by a German school leader).

Inductive and deductive

Deductive studies start from a set of first principles. They start from what we know about leadership, drawing on managerial wisdom, folklore, moral precepts, psychological truisms, sometimes with reference to empirical research, sometimes not. Much early literature took this form. There were seminal writings on leadership, 'doctrines of the great educators', philosophical treatises on the nature of the art.

Pronouncements of politicians often seem to have this 'first principles' flavour, sometimes a wish list comprising what is taken to be the unarguable character of leadership. Lists of competencies may be compiled by a working party of selected heads, policy advisers, or teachers, drawing on experience, common sense, or an analysis of what the job entails.

Such studies are not necessarily any less valid or useful than inductive studies, but the latter often throw up findings which are unexpected and take common sense by surprise. Inductive studies typically begin with a study of people who are regarded as effective leaders, examining what it is that makes them tick. An example of this is the classic study by Howard Gardner of great world leaders, entitled *Leading Minds* (1995). In it he infers a number of common features of outstanding leaders, such as a willingness to confront authority, risk-taking, resilience in the face of failure, and confidence in one's own instinct and intuition.

Gardner's approach is similar to that adopted by Hay–McBer (2000) in their work for the Department for Education and Employment (DFEE).

Figure 8.1 Drawing depicting leadership

While Gardner inferred his leadership characteristics from reading and second-hand sources, Hay–McBer took a step closer to the real thing by the use of face-to-face interviews with leaders themselves. On the basis of these interviews, together with data from those on the receiving end, researchers derived a set of competencies (with an 'i') distinguishing these *people qualities* from the *job competences*. The distinction between competences (no 'i') and competencies is more than an academic nicety. Describing the requirements of the task is quite different from assessing the qualities, or 'competencies' which someone may bring with them – sometimes idiosyncratic, particularistic, often larger than life.

A recent Hay–McBer study, *Lessons for Leadership* (2001) comparing selected school leaders and their counterparts in the business world found that educational leaders outshone their business counterparts on most major traits except that of delegation. Even the most successful heads held on to power more and delegated less than their peers in the commercial world.

Subjective and objective

The source of evidence on leadership may be leaders themselves, providing their own subjective accounts of what they do, how they spend their time, or what they perceive as their own qualities or competencies. This is sometimes approached through a 'behavioural event' interview in which the researcher tries to 'walk' the interviewee back through some real event recently experienced. The interviewer prompts the interviewee by trying to illuminate the minute detail of time and place: 'Was it raining that morning?', 'What did you do after you hung up your umbrella?', 'What were your first thoughts?' Recollections may be coloured, distorted or transformed in hindsight so, however powerful this methodology, it is useful to include accounts from other, more disinterested, sources. Interviewing others with knowledge of the person in question – teachers, parents, authority personnel – also renders subjective accounts which may be equally coloured by personal recollection and predisposition. However, the intent is, through a triangulation of different subjectivities, to arrive at a more 'objective' or balanced account.

Sources of evidence may be 'objective' in a harder sense when they rest on more or less indisputable measures. We can measure the amount of time a head actually spends in school, in the community or in classrooms. We can compute who he or she spends their time with: with pupils, with parents, with teachers, in national committees. We can measure numbers of phone calls, emails, letters and their sources. We can gauge, with some degree of accuracy, the number of decisions someone makes in the course of a day. These data do not always square with the leader's own first-hand report of what he or she did, but as we have found in a number of studies, the juxtaposition of subjective recollection and objective record can provide a rich source of data.

Behaviourist and constructivist

For years and decades, indeed half a century, behaviourist and constructivist schools have argued their corners. A pure behaviourist approach rests on the belief that all that really matters is what we can observe. Behaviourists have little interest in what leaders think, or think they think. What they want to know is what leaders actually do. It follows, therefore, that bringing about change means quite simply changing people's behaviour. Thinking and feeling will follow on. At the other extreme, a pure constructivist approach rests on the belief that behaviour is only understandable when we have access to the thought and feeling that 'construct' behaviour. Reality is not 'out there' but 'in here', in the imagination of the individual. What matters is how leaders make sense of their own world and can, with a changed world view, change their behaviour.

In evaluation it is rare for people to adopt such purist positions, but the two underlying philosophies do lend themselves to different methods of collecting data. A focus on behaviour favours systematic observation techniques, rating scales and plenty of training for those who use them. OFSTED inspections rely fairly heavily on observation of what teachers do, and the ultimate grade given to a teacher represents a compilation of observable behaviours such as introducing, questioning, explaining, naming (but never shaming) and controlling. Shadowing a teacher over the course of a day is not within the OFSTED repertoire but is used fruitfully by researchers with an interest in how behaviour changes according to context, age of pupils or topic taught. Video footage of a day in the life of a school leader, or of a single leadership event, may be the most faithful source for cataloguing behaviour.

From a constructivist point of view we would have to issue a caution over the use of video as objective behavioural evidence. Any item of video footage is contained within a frame: that frame is dictated by the camera position or the selective pointing of the camera by the person shooting the scene. What is just outside the frame may be what helps to explain and interpret behaviour. And how the subject of the video clip 'frames' the incident himself or herself may be the most telling evidence from an evaluator's standpoint. So 'framing' becomes an important concept in exploring the inner-world of leadership, and 'reframing' is important in formative evaluation because it helps leaders to see things through a different lens, which in turn leads to a change in behaviour. Leadership is understood, then, not as a finished product but as something existing in a state of continuous transition.

SUGGESTION:

Think of a leader you admire. This may be someone in your school or someone you know from another context.
Consider what behaviours he or she exhibits that lead you to make that judgement.
Consider the relationship between what he/she 'is' and what he/she 'does' that leads you to that judgement.
What aspects of that person are transferable to others? What can you learn from that person?

Uses in self-evaluation

Tools and strategies used by researchers to explore leadership lend themselves well to self-evaluation, as long as the cautions and caveats discussed above are kept in mind. Critical friends and experts should be called on to assist with technical matters such as questionnaire construction, interview protocols, observational schedules and training, as appropriate.

Table 8.1 provides references for some qualitative and quantitative studies on leadership which may be a useful reference point in terms of both content and methodology.

What are we learning about leadership?

What have we learned and what are we learning from this large and diverse body of studies? Taken as a whole, studies tend to converge on a number of leadership qualities such as:

- Providing direction and strategic vision;
- Taking and sharing decisions;
- Listening and responding to staff, parents' and pupils' concerns;
- Supporting and developing staff;
- Recognising and celebrating good practice;
- Maintaining an information flow;
- Planning and budgeting;
- Devolving responsibility and encouraging leadership of others;
- Promoting the school in the local and wider community.

Table 8.1 Quantitative and qualitative studies of leadership

| **LEADERS AS SOURCE** | | **OTHERS AS SOURCE** | |
Behaviour	*Identity*	*Behaviour*	*Identity*
Quantitative	Mortimore et al. (1988) Cheng (1996) Van der Grift (2000)	Van der Grift (2000) Hay-McBer (2000)	Leithwood et al. (1993) MacBeath et al. (1998)
Qualitative	Bryk et al. (1986) Chapman (1992) Southworth (1995)	Hall (1994) Dimmock (1996) Dempster and Mahoney (1998) Sergiovanni (2001)	Day et al. (2000) Moos et al. (2000)

Few would disagree with these broad principles, but there is also a dissenting strand in the literature, offering a counter to the prescriptive one-size-fits-all approach to leadership. In an earlier book in this series, *Leadership* (2001), Tom Sergiovanni offers this counsel:

> It is not by chance that some leaders are more effective than others, even when all are faced with similar demands and constraints. Effective leaders have a better understanding of how the worlds of schooling and of leadership work. They have figured out alternatives to direct leadership that are better able to get people connected to each other and to their work and to their responsibilities. They are less likely to base their practice on the assumption that predetermined solutions exist for most of the problems they face. . . . Yielding to practicality, these effective leaders realise the most important problems are beyond the reach of easy answers often embedded in the technical and rational solutions offered by distant central authorities or embedded in the rhetoric of simplistically conceived school reform.
>
> (p. 3)

This emphasis on broad principles but working out one's own salvation in a particular context, receives support from a recent international study of Danish, English, Norwegian and Irish headteachers (Moos, 2000). It provides valuable insights on the way in which school leaders construct their identity as leaders: over time, *becoming* different people in the job as they respond to different people's responses to them, to changing expectations and to changing social and political contexts.

The study also provided a salutary reminder of the nature of evidence. Although researchers were at pains to establish a climate of trust and confidentiality, what school leaders chose to disclose depended in part on the sex and status of the interviewer and interviewee. When interview transcripts were fed back to interviewees, although faithful in factual detail, they often did not ring true with the interviewee because written accounts are not the same as verbal face-to-face accounts, which are embedded in context and modulated by tone, pause, inflexion, and body language.

Leadership and headship

Much of the literature tends to treat leadership and headship as synonymous – a very British phenomenon, as many of our European colleagues observe. It reflects a deeply institutionalised school culture in which staff, parents, authorities and public look to the head to turn things round. This view is reflected in the language not just of a popular press but of educational journals. In a review of the Government's *Fresh Start in Managing Schools Today* (September 2000) the lead article refers to the 'reign' of a headteacher who had 'turned round a troubled school in Fyfe (*sic*)'. It is, of course, a central tenet of the Fresh Start philosophy and generally seen in all UK countries as the single most important lever to improve schools and raise standards.

With headship accorded such a powerful place, and so deeply embedded in Government policy, it provides an obvious starting point for self-evaluation. Without self-reflective and self-critical heads and management teams how can leadership become more of a shared enterprise? How can teachers be expected to be open to self-critique and how can the organisation become a real community of learners and leaders?

How good am I as a leader? 'Me as I am'

The counsel to 'know thyself' offers a good place to begin. But it can not be undertaken lightly as true self-discovery shines light into areas which we might often prefer to ignore. 'What kind of leader am I?' is not easily divorced from the deeper questions, 'What kind of a person am I?' and

'What is the discrepancy between what I present to others and who I really "am"?' 'Is there a true "authentic self" or only self-in-context?'

One way into these questions is through the 'Me as I am' instrument (Figure 8.2). It sets out a list of qualities, competencies and attitudes each with their polar opposites, asking the individual respondent to assess himself or herself in relation to these. As it is an individual and confidential exercise, dishonesty and dissimulation can only be in relation to one's self. And even if the 'I' is tempted to cheat on the 'me' it is unlikely to be done without a certain degree of discomfort and recognition of the inherent self-deception.

In our experience headteachers, and others, like this instrument. They often express surprise at the 'findings', as if they had been researchers uncovering new unsuspected data. While the exercise is unlikely to reveal new undiscovered aspects of self, the choice of terminology and the focus on specific words can provoke unaccustomed ways of thinking and seeing. Headteachers often report having new insights about themselves and find a useful working profile beginning to emerge from the analysis.

Typically, people report that they have to puzzle over the items because how they respond depends on the context. I may be confident in one context but lacking in confidence in another. I may be organised in school but disorganised at home. I may be a good listener with my peers but a poor listener when it comes to pupils, or especially with pupils that I have already categorised as troublemakers.

There are resonances here with the four-country study of identity described above. Identity is not only in flux over time, being shaped and reshaped by events but also by context and conditions. This recognition of contextual effects is perhaps the most important insight of all because it leads to an awareness of who we 'are' in different places and relationships and how these shape how we think and feel and how we respond to others. In her book *The Power of Place* Winifred Gallagher (1993) draws on a substantive body of evidence to illustrate how much we are the products of *where* we are:

> . . . while we readily accept that a healthy seed can't grow into a plant without the right soil, light, and water, and that a feral dog won't behave like a pet, we resist recognizing the importance of environment in our own lives.

(p. 16)

rule-breaker	1	2	3	4	5	rule-observer
efficient	1	2	3	4	5	inefficient
radical	1	2	3	4	5	conservative
share power	1	2	3	4	5	hold power
authoritarian	1	2	3	4	5	democratic
charismatic	1	2	3	4	5	reserved
pursue long-term goals	1	2	3	4	5	pursue short-term goals
forgiving	1	2	3	4	5	unforgiving
competitive	1	2	3	4	5	uncompetitive
delegate a lot	1	2	3	4	5	delegate very little
like change	1	2	3	4	5	dislike change
confront bad practice	1	2	3	4	5	tolerate bad practice
gentle	1	2	3	4	5	tough
reliable	1	2	3	4	5	erratic
strong values	1	2	3	4	5	open-minded
attend to detail	1	2	3	4	5	careless about detail
gregarious	1	2	3	4	5	private
size up people well	1	2	3	4	5	bad at sizing up people
demanding	1	2	3	4	5	undemanding
individualistic	1	2	3	4	5	team player
inflexible	1	2	3	4	5	flexible
optimist	1	2	3	4	5	pessimist
fight for beliefs	1	2	3	4	5	back off from a fight
entrepreneurial	1	2	3	4	5	cautious
predictable	1	2	3	4	5	unpredictable
take risks	1	2	3	4	5	avoid risks
take decisions easily	1	2	3	4	5	difficulty in decision-making
assertive	1	2	3	4	5	unassertive
manipulative	1	2	3	4	5	straightforward
easily influenced	1	2	3	4	5	unbending
low profile	1	2	3	4	5	high profile
idealistic	1	2	3	4	5	pragmatic
listen more than talk	1	2	3	4	5	talk more than listen
lead from the front	1	2	3	4	5	lead from the back

Figure 8.2 'Me as I am'

This understanding of the power of place is of crucial importance for the exercise of leadership, not simply because it helps to interpret one's behaviour but because it leads to a deeper understanding of how and why pupils, staff and parents behave they way they do in certain situations. It becomes even more powerful when self-evaluation instruments are entrusted to others to complete on our behalf. In the course of a recent leadership academy in Germany, one headteacher reported that he had asked his staff to evaluate him and was surprised to discover that a good number of his staff circled a '1' describing him as 'gentle' rather than 'tough'. He had never considered himself to be 'gentle'. In the ensuing discussion with his colleagues it became clear that while he was 'tough' in many situations, there were also times where he displayed gentleness and care in dealing with difficult situations, particularly those involving people.

Such revelations can be both affirming and challenging. They set in train a process which can lead in many directions and to many different places. They validate the instrument and its potential uses at different levels and in different contexts in the school.

We can take this a step further by comparing the 'Me as I am' with 'Me as I would like to be' (Figure 8.3). The structure and content of the items are the same as before but with a different focus, a different mindset. The surprise this time round is that the ideal self is rarely 'ideal' or predictable. People do not necessarily choose to be more organised, more assertive or better listeners. Sensitive people sometimes wish they were less sensitive. Efficient people occasionally wish they could be less efficient. Rule-observers sometimes say they would like to have the courage to be more of a rule-breaker.

In the leadership academy mentioned above, several school leaders circled a '3' (and sometimes a '4') in the 'tolerate bad practice'/'confront bad practice' column but circled a '1' when it came to 'Me as I would like to be'. This was not only revealing but an important entrée into the discussion of causes, consequences and contexts. When is it necessary to confront bad practice? And when should it be ignored? How is it done most effectively? Where do we get the courage and skill to do it? What can we learn from others who have rated themselves good at it?

The 'Me as I am' instrument may be used by leaders in the privacy of their own offices or classrooms, but its maximum benefit derives from the variety of perspectives and multiplicity of contexts. It can be used in

rule-breaker	1	2	3	4	5	rule-observer
efficient	1	2	3	4	5	inefficient
radical	1	2	3	4	5	conservative
share power	1	2	3	4	5	hold power
authoritarian	1	2	3	4	5	democratic
charismatic	1	2	3	4	5	reserved
forgiving	1	2	3	4	5	unforgiving
competitive	1	2	3	4	5	uncompetitive
delegate a lot	1	2	3	4	5	delegate very little
like change	1	2	3	4	5	dislike change
confront bad practice	1	2	3	4	5	tolerate bad practice
gentle	1	2	3	4	5	tough
reliable	1	2	3	4	5	erratic
strong values	1	2	3	4	5	open-minded
attend to detail	1	2	3	4	5	careless about detail
gregarious	1	2	3	4	5	private
size up people well	1	2	3	4	5	bad at sizing up people
demanding	1	2	3	4	5	undemanding
individualistic	1	2	3	4	5	team player
inflexible	1	2	3	4	5	flexible
optimist	1	2	3	4	5	pessimist
fight for beliefs	1	2	3	4	5	back off from a fight
entrepreneurial	1	2	3	4	5	cautious
predictable	1	2	3	4	5	unpredictable
pursue long-term goals	1	2	3	4	5	pursue short-term goals
take risks	1	2	3	4	5	avoid risks
take decisions easily	1	2	3	4	5	difficulty in decision-making
assertive	1	2	3	4	5	unassertive
manipulative	1	2	3	4	5	straightforward
easily influenced	1	2	3	4	5	unbending
low profile	1	2	3	4	5	high profile
idealistic	1	2	3	4	5	pragmatic
listen more than talk	1	2	3	4	5	talk more than listen
lead from the front	1	2	3	4	5	lead from the back

Figure 8.3 'Me as I would like to be'

paired work with a colleague or mentor or with a 'critical friend' to talk through the findings, broadening the discussion to an evaluation which goes beyond individual qualities to impact on the school.

We know of courageous leaders who have given the instrument to colleagues – the senior management team or heads of department, asking them to complete the inventory anonymously. Having done so, it meets a number of objectives:

• Provides feedback and opens up discussion;
• Generates trust and goodwill among staff;
• Models for staff a process they can undertake themselves;
• Moves discussion from individual quality to organisational impact.

SUGGESTION:

The instrument provides a template which can be adapted to many different contexts and purposes, for example for pupils, for evaluation of teaching and learning, or (as we showed in chapter 5) for evaluating school ethos and culture.
Consider ways in which you might adapt and customise the instrument to other contexts in your own school.

However interesting the self-portrait that emerges from 'Me as I am', leaders are ultimately accountable for what they do rather than for what they are and, as their colleagues might insist, 'by their deeds shall we know them'.

What impact do I/we have on the school?
Key questions

As we move from personal qualities to impact on the school, the effectiveness of leadership becomes the focus of evaluation. If the ability to confront bad practice is at a premium it should be reflected in how people behave and the strategies employed in addressing the issues. If being a good listener is a significant quality of leadership, it should be reflected in a staff's willingness to speak out and to feel valued. If being democratic is important, it should be reflected in the effective functioning of the organisation and its ability to enhance the achievement of all pupils and staff.

In other words, how are personal qualities translated into policies and practices which ensure that there is continuous improvement? What impact does the leader have on the school and individual pupil performance? And how is that measured relative to other schools, other leaders?

In Scotland, the document '*How Good is Our School?*' (1996) is now used by all schools to evaluate all facets of their practice. During its half-decade of use it has moved progressively from a peripheral, and even irksome, imposition to a more integral and welcome place within ongoing school life and development planning. Once viewed as the province of senior management, it is now more and more seen as relevant to all staff. Of the thirty-three in the suite of indicators one focuses specifically on leadership and management.

Figure 8.4 illustrates the indicator contained in the document. It sets out the three key themes of the indicator and then goes on to exemplify what a level 4 (a performance with major weaknesses) would look like, and a level 2, which describes a performance with more strengths than weaknesses. This leaves it to the school itself to devise a level 1 and a level 3. These four categories are then used to rate leadership and management – by leaders themselves and by those who are subject to their leadership. Figure 8.5 shows an evaluation tool that allows individual professional qualities to be assessed one by one, providing a profile of skills.

Once again, the benefits of this instrument are enhanced when a 'critical friend' is involved, supporting, probing and pressing for evidence. As Gus Macdonald, a Scottish head, wrote (in MacBeath, 1998), we don't always know what we know or know what we don't know, and it can take an external source, and enlightened eye, to help us to recognise our own blind spots.

This instrument may also be used collaboratively with senior staff, with the management team for example, going through the self-evaluation instrument together, changing the 'I' to 'we', underlining the point that leadership extends beyond the headteacher and is a joint responsibility.

Level 4 Illustration

- He or she demonstrates a high level of professional competence and commitment based on wide-ranging up-to-date knowledge and skills, including the ability to initiate, direct, communicate, manage staff and their development and delegate effectively. Where applicable, his or her teaching is a model of good practice.
- He or she has a wide range of relevant personal qualities, including the ability to create confidence and inspire others; he or she is a positive influence on his or her area of responsibility. He or she has the ability to evaluate objectively the qualities of staff and their contributions to teamwork. He or she demonstrates breadth of vision and can take difficult decisions effectively when necessary.
- He or she has very good relationships with pupils, parents and staff. There is a planned development of teamwork, staff are involved in policy development and his or her dissemination of information is clear and prompt.

A performance broadly equivalent to that illustrated above would merit a Level 4 award.

Level 2 Illustration

- He or she demonstrates a degree of professional competence based on relevant knowledge, although this is not always successfully applied in practical contexts. There are difficulties in communicating and/or delegating effectively and attempts at initiating and directing are only partially effective. Where applicable, their teaching provides a good model in a number of respects.
- He or she demonstrates leadership but is not wholly successful in inspiring confidence in others and a number of staff do not respond to his or her management style, either because he or she is not wholly successful in inspiring confidence or does not provide a clear sense of direction. He or she lacks breadth of vision and tends to avoid difficult decisions.
- Difficulties arise at times in his or her relationships with pupils, staff and/or parents. He or she has difficulties at times in creating a team approach and while there are attempts to do so, in practice there are only occasional instances of effective teamwork and dissemination of information is not always clear or prompt.

A performance broadly equivalent to that illustrated above would merit a Level 2 award.

Figure 8.4 How good is leadership in our school?

Rate yourself on a four-point scale (1–4) in terms of each of the leadership qualities (4 = very good, 3 = good, 2 = fair, 1 = unsatisfactory).

In the final column, identify up to 3 aspects in which you would like to set personal and/or professional goals.

Qualities of Leadership	1	2	3	4	*Goals* *
• *Professional competence and commitment*					
Commitment					
Up-to-date knowledge					
Ability to initiate					
Ability to direct					
Communication skills					
Manage staff effectively					
Support staff development					
Delegates effectively					
Models good teacher					
• *Leadership qualities*					
Creates confidence in others					
Inspires others					
Has a positive impact on practice					
Ability to evaluate others effectively					
Demonstrates breadth of vision					
Takes decisions effectively					
• *Relationship with people and deployment of teamwork*					
Maintains good relationships with staff					
Maintains good relationships with pupils					
Maintains good relationship with parents					
Involves others in policy development					
Disseminates information promptly and effectively					

Figure 8.5 Qualities of leadership – self-rating

Role play and rehearsal

A useful approach is for the head to role-play a situation in which searching questions are being put to him or her by an external evaluator, say a school inspector or the director of education or the chair of governors. These may include, for example:

- What impact do I/we have on the morale and commitment of staff?
- What impact do I/we have on the quality of learning and teaching?
- Is the quality of learning and teaching improving in the school?
- How do we compare with other schools?
- How has the school, and sections of the school, performed this year compared to last year?
- Is there an improvement across all sections of the school? And where is the evidence?

Schools in England preparing for inspection are advised to rehearse the issues with reference to the OFSTED Framework, which suggests the following criteria, or indicators:

- Leadership ensures clear direction for the work and development of the school, and promotes high standards;
- The school has explicit aims and values, including a commitment to good relationships and equality of opportunity for all, which are reflected in all its work;
- There is rigorous monitoring, evaluation and development of teaching;
- There is effective appraisal and performance management;
- The school identifies appropriate priorities and targets, takes the necessary action, and reviews progress towards them;
- There is a shared commitment to improvement and the capacity to succeed;
- Governors fulfil their statutory duties in helping to shape the direction of the school and have a good understanding of its strengths and weaknesses;
- Educational priorities are supported through careful financial management;
- Good delegation ensures the effective contribution of staff with management responsibilities.

As many of these criteria illustrate, management and leadership have less to do with the qualities of the individual or team than the effect on the school as a whole – its efficiency, strategic approach and general well-being. OFSTED also advises that as well as the headteacher, every 'governor, and member of staff who carries some co-ordination or management responsibility for an aspect of the school's work, should, from time to time, assess how well they are doing and provide the evidence to back up their views'. We would go further and suggest that evaluation of school leadership and management should be an integral part of the school self-evaluation culture described in chapter 2. Self-evaluating leaders and learning schools need less time for rehearsal and role play because they are prepared for external scrutiny at any time and welcome the challenging visitor. We would also add that it is not only those within the formal management hierarchy who should be engaged in such evaluative activities but all those with a stake in effective learning and teaching.

The density of leadership

Tom Sergiovanni (2001) has coined the term 'density of leadership' as a measure of how far leadership roles extend within a school. As a proportion of the school population, how many teachers or pupils have such roles and how many would recognise their own leadership positions? How much informal leadership is exercised by people to whom you turn for help and guidance, whom you would rely on in a crisis? Who do you trust to represent your position to others? Who are most effective at presenting the case for the opposition?

We often tend to look at management and leadership in terms of structural functions although we know, intuitively at least, that what often counts most takes place within the informal culture of the school. The chair of the board of governors may have the structural position, but leadership may come from another member of the board. A union rep may have an influential role in the formal structure, but may not be a source of leadership within the informal culture. Departmental heads may be efficient managers but not leaders. Unpromoted teachers may have little formal leadership role but exert a powerful influence in informal relationships. We can think of individual pupils who are virtually powerless within the formal structure but are influential leaders within

the informal culture. Prefects and school captains may have some structural power but not be seen as leaders by their peers.

QUESTIONS:

In your own school or organisation, what proportion of the staff
have leadership roles?
What proportion of the pupils or students do so?
Who else exercises leadership?
In the two boxes in Figure 8.6 you might like to enter the names
of people who play a leadership role in the formal structure and in
the informal culture.

Formal	*Informal*

Figure 8.6 Formal and informal leadership

Leaders often are seen as operating from the apex of their organisations. On the other hand, they may locate themselves at the centre of
a web of relationships. They are occasionally followers, taking their lead
from others. From time to time they share leadership and provide
opportunities for others to lead. In all of these contexts evaluation is
critical, not simply because it tells about how effective different strategies
are but because it alerts us to the need for change and opens our eyes to
how different things might be.

References

Argyris, C. (1993) *Knowledge for Action: A Guide to Overcoming Barriers to Organizational Change*, San Francisco: Jossey-Bass.

Arnot, M. (1982) 'Male hegemony, social class and women's education', in *Journal of Education*, 164(1), 64–69.

Arnot, M. and Reay, D. (2001) *New Constructions of Student Voice*, Paper delivered at the American Educational Research Association, Seattle (April).

Barber, M. (2001) 'High expectations and education for all, no matter what: creating a world-class education service in England' in M. Fielding, *Taking Education Really Seriously: Four Years' Hard Labour*, London: Routledge.

Bennett, M. (2001) 'School Inspection in Scotland', unpublished doctoral thesis, University of Strathclyde.

Binney, G. and Williams, W. (1997) *Leaning into the Future: Changing the Way People Change Organisations*, London: Nicholas Brealey.

Broadhead, P. (1995) 'Changing practice: primary professional development explained', in *Cambridge Journal of Education* 25(3) (November), 315–26.

Brookover, W. et al. (1979) *School Social Systems and Student Achievement; Schools Can Make a Difference*, New York: Praeger.

Bryk, A. S., Lee., V. and Holland, P. (1993) *Catholic Schools and the Common Good*, Cambridge, Mass.: Harvard University Press.

Bryk, A., Sebring, P., Kerbow, D., Rollow, S. and Easton, J. (1996) *Charting Chicago School Reform*, Boulder, Colorado: Westview Press.

Campbell, C., Gillborn, D., Sammons, P., Wareen, S. and Whitty, G. (2001), 'Inclusive Schooling' in *NSIN Research Matters*, London: Institute of Education.

Chapman, J. D. (1992) 'Making substance the leading edge of executive work: towards a more integrated approach for understanding leadership, school-based decision-making and school effectiveness', in C. Dimmock (ed.) *Leadership, School-Based Decision-making and School Effectiveness*.

Chelimsky, E. and Shadish, W. (1999) *Evaluation for the 21st Century: A Handbook*, London: Sage.

Cheng, Y.C. (1996) 'Principal leadership as a critical indicator of school performance: Evidence from multi-levels of primary schools', in *School Effectiveness
and School Improvement* (5), 299–317.

Cheng, Y.C. (1999) 'The pursuit of school effectiveness and educational quality
in Hong Kong', in *School Effectiveness and School Improvement* 10(1) (March).

Claxton, G. (2000) *The Intuitive Practitioner: On the Value of Not Always Knowing What
One is Doing*, Buckingham: Open University Press.

Cousins, B. (1996) 'Understanding organizational learning for leadership and
school improvement' in K. Leithwood, J. Chapman, D. Corson, P. Hallinger,
A. Hart, *International Handbook of Educational Leadership and Administration*,
589–652, Dordrecht: Kluwer.

Covey, S. (1994a) *First Things First*, New York: Simon & Schuster.

—— (1994b) *Principle-Centred Leadership*, New York: Houghton Mifflin.

Csikszentmihalyi, M. (1990) *Flow: the Psychology of Optimal Experience*, New York:
HarperCollins.

Csikszentmihalyi, M. (1996) *Creativity*, New York: HarperCollins.

Csikszentmihalyi, M., Rathunde, K. and Whalen, S. (1998) *Talented Teenagers*,
New York: Cambridge University Press.

Cullingford, C. (1999) (ed.) *An Inspector Calls: OFSTED and its Effects on School
Standards*, London: Kogan Page.

Dalin, P. with Gunther-Rolff, H.G. (1993) *Changing the School Culture*, London:
Cassell.

Dalin, P. and Rust, V.D. (1996) *Towards Schooling for the Twenty-First Century*,
London: Cassell.

Dannaway, Y. (2001) 'Should we sugar-coat the truth then, Miss?', Unpublished
M.ED paper, Faculty of Education, University of Cambridge.

Darling-Hammond, L. (1995) *Authentic Assessment in Action*, New York: Teachers'
College Press.

Day, C., Harris, A., Hadfield, M., Toley, H. and Beresford, J. (2000) *Leading
Schools in Times of Change*, Buckingham: Open University Press.

Dempster, N. and Mahoney, P. (1998) 'Ethical challenges in school leadership'
in J. McBeath (ed.) *Effective School Leadership: Responding to Change*, London: Paul
Chapman.

Department for Education and Skills (2001) *Excellence in Schools*, London:
DfES.

Department of Education for Northern Ireland (2000) *Education and Training
Inspectorate: Evaluation of Inspection 1996–98*, Belfast, DENI.

DFEE (1999) *School Teachers' Pay and Conditions*, London: Department for
Education and Employment.

—— (1999) *Fresh Start*, London: Department for Education and Employment.

Dimmock, C. (1996) 'Dilemmas for school leaders and administrators in
restructuring', in K. Leithwood, J. Chapman, D. Corson, P. Hallinger and

A. Hart (eds.) *International Handbook of Educational Leadership and Administration I*, Kluwer: Dordrecht.

Eisner, E. (1991) *The Enlightened Eye*, New York: Macmillan.

European Commission (2000) *European Report on Quality of Education*, Paper presented to European Ministers, Budapest (June).

Fidler, B. and Earley, P. (2001) *Improving Schools and Inspection*, London: Paul Chapman.

Fielding, M. (1998) *Making a Difference*, Paper presented at International Congress on School Effectiveness and School Improvement, Manchester.

—— (1999) *Students as Radical Agents of Change: a Three-Year Case Study*, Paper presented at British Educational Research Association, University of Sussex (September).

—— (ed.) (2001) *Taking Education Really Seriously: Four Years' Hard Labour*, London: Routledge.

Frost, D. (2001) Unpublished questionnaire for the Hertfordshire-Cambridge University Learning Partnership.

Gallagher, W. (1993) *The Power of Place*, New York: Praeger.

Gardener, H. (1995) *Leading Minds: An Anatomy of Leadership*, London: HarperCollins

Gray, J. (1988) 'The Contribution of Educational Research to the Cause of School Improvement', professional lecture, Institute of Education, London University.

Hall, V. (1994) *Making it Happen; a Study of Women Headteachers of Primary and Secondary Schools in England and Wales*, New Orleans (April): American Educational Research Association.

Hampden-Turner, C. and Trompenaars, F. (1993) *The Seven Cultures of Capitalism*, Doubleday: New York.

Hargreaves, D. H. (1967) *Social Relations in a Secondary School*, London: Routledge & Kegan Paul.

Herndon, J. (1968), *The Way it Spozed to Be*, New York: Wiley.

House, E. (1973) *School Evaluation: The Politics and Process*, San Francisco: McCutcheon.

Illich, I. (1971) *Deschooling Society*, New York: Harper and Row, in England and Wales: Education Management Information Exchange.

International Network for Innovative Schools and School Systems (2000) *The Self-evaluation Toolbox*, Gutersloh: Bertelsmann Foundation.

Kounin, J.S. (1970) *Discipline and Group Management in Classrooms*, New York: Holt, Rhinehart, Winston.

Learmonth, J. (2000) *Inspection: What's in it for Schools?*, London: Falmer Routledge.

Lee, B. (2001) 'OFSTED and the impact of special measures', in *Education Review* 14(2), 68–74, London: National Union of Teachers.

Leithwood, K., Begley, P.T. and Cousins, B. (1993) *Developing Expert Leadership for Effective Schools*, London: RoutledgeFalmer.

Leithwood, K., Edge, K., Jantzi, D. (1999) *Educational Accountability: the State of the Art*, Gutersloh: Bertelsmann Foundation.

Leone, C.M. and Richards, M.H. (1989) 'Classwork and homework in early adolescence: the ecology of achievement', in *Journal of Youth and Adolescence* 18(6), 531–49.

Leeuw, F. (2001) *Reciprocity and the Evaluation of Educational Quality; Assumptions and Reality Checks*, Keynote paper for the European Union Congress, Karlstat: Sweden (April 2–4).

Lings, P. and Desforges, C. (1999) 'On subject differences in applying knowledge to learn', in *Research Papers in Education* 14 (2), 199–221.

Little, J.W. (1990) 'Teachers as colleagues', in A. Liebermann (ed.) *Schools as Collaborative Cultures: Creating the Future Now*, Basingstoke: Falmer.

Louis, K. S. (1994) 'Beyond managed change: Rethinking how schools improve', in *School Effectiveness and School Improvement*, I (1), 2–24.

Louis, K.S. and Miles, M.B. (1990) *Improving the Urban High School: What Works and Why*, London: Cassell.

Luan, T.K.S. (1997) 'Students' reports of their cognitive processes and level of understanding during regular classroom instructions', in J. Tan, S. Gopinathan, and H. W. Kam, *Education in Singapore*, 187–207, Singapore: Prentice-Hall.

MacBeath, J. (1993) 'The threefold path to enlightenment', *Times Educational Supplement*, 15 September, p. 25.

MacBeath, J., Kruchov, C., Riley, K. (1994) *Images of Leadership*, Glasgow: University of Strathclyde.

MacBeath, J., Boyd, B., Rand, J. and Bell, S. (1995) *Schools Speak for Themselves*, London: National Union of Teachers.

MacBeath, J. (1998) (ed.) *Effective School Leadership: Responding to Change*, London: Paul Chapman/Sage.

MacBeath, J. (1999) *Schools Must Speak for Themselves*, London: Routledge.

MacBeath, J., Jakobsen, L., Meuret, D., Schratz, M. (2000) *Self-evaluation in European Schools: a Story of Change*, London: Routledge.

MacBeath, J. and Mortimore, P. (2001) *Improving School Effectiveness*, Buckingham: Open University Press.

MacGilchrist, B., Mortimore, P., Savage, J. and Beresford, C. (1995) *Planning Matters*, London: Paul Chapman.

McBride, B. (2001) 'Inspection in Scotland', in *Education Review* 14(2), 58–64, London: National Union of Teachers.

McGlynn, A. and Stalker, H. (1995) 'Recent developments in the Scottish process of school inspection', *Cambridge Journal of Education* 25 (1): 13–21.

McGlynn, A. (2000) *Accountability in Education: Making it Happen in 11 School Systems*, International Network of Innovative Schools and School Systems, Gutersloh: Bertelsmann Foundation.

Mirza, H. S. (1992) *Young, Black and Female*, London: Routledge.

Mitchell, K. (2001) 'Inspection: why, how, for whom, by whom – and where next?' in *Education Review* 14(2), 30–37, London: National Union of Teachers.

Mitchell, C. and Sackney, L. (2000) *Profound Improvement: Building Capacity for a Learning Community*, Lisse: Swets and Zeitlinger.

Moos, L. (2000) 'Global and national perspectives on leadership', in Riley, K.A., and Lewis, K.S., *Leadership for Change and School Reform*, London: Routledge.

Mortimore, P., Sammons, P., Stroll, L., Lewis, D., Ecob, R. (1989) *School Matters*, London: Open Books.

Myers, K. (2000) (ed.) *Whatever Happened to Equal Opportunities?* London: Routledge.

OECD (2000) *Education at a Glance: OECD Indicators*, Paris: OECD.

OFSTED (2000) *The Handbook for the Inspection of Schools*, London: OFSTED.

Osler, D. (1999) Keynote address for the Edinburgh Education Authority Annual Conference (unpublished), Edinburgh, UK (September).

Reay, D. (1998) *Class Work: Mothers' Involvement in Their Children's Primary Schooling*, London: University College Press.

Ross, S. (1995) 'Using Ethos Indicators in a Primary School', in *Managing Schools Today*, 26–30.

Rudduck, J. R. and Wallace, G. (eds.) (1995) *School Improvement: What Can Pupils Tell Us?* London: David Fulton.

Rutter, M., Maughan, B., Mortimore, P. and Ouston, J. (1979) *Fifteen Thousand Hours: Secondary Schools and Their Effects on Children*, London: Open Books.

Sammons, P., Hillman, J. and Mortimore, P. (1994) *Key Characteristics of Effective Schools: A Review of School Effectiveness Research*, London: Office of Standards in Education.

Sarason, S.B. (1986) *The Culture of the School and the Problem of Change*, Boston: Allyn and Bacon.

Saunders, L. (2001) *Evaluating School Self-evaluation*, London: National Foundation for Educational Research.

Scottish Office Education Department (1992a) *Using Ethos Indicators in Primary School Self-Evaluation: Taking Account of the Views of Pupils, Parents and Teachers*, Edinburgh: HM Inspectors of Schools (HMSO).

—— (1992b) *Interchange No 11 Performance Indicators and Examination Results*, Research and Intelligence Unit, Edinburgh: Scottish Office Education Department.

Scottish Office Education and Industry Department (1996) *How Good is Our School?* HM Inspectors of Schools, Edinburgh: Scottish Office Education and Industry Department.

—— (1998) *Standards and Quality 1995–1998, A report by HM Inspectors of Schools*, Audit Unit, Edinburgh: Scottish Office Education Department.

Senge, P. (1990) *The Fifth Discipline: The Art and Practice of the Learning Organisation*, New York: Doubleday.

Sergiovanni, T. (2001) *Leadership: What's in it for schools?*, London: RoutledgeFalmer.

Southworth, G. (1995), *Looking into Primary Headship: A Research-Based Interpretation*, London: Falmer.

Standing International Conference of Central and General Inspectors of Education (undated), Inspectorates of Education in Europe, Utrecht: SICI.

Steiner-Löffler, U. (1996) *Pupils Evaluate School Culture: a Photographic Approach*, Paper delivered at the European Educational Research Association, Seville (September).

Tay-Koayeiuw Luan (1997) 'Students' reports of their cognitive processes and level of understanding during regular classroom instruction' in J. Tan, S. Gopi Nathan Ho Wah Kam, *Education in Singapore*, pp. 187–204, Singapore: Prentice Hall.

The Third International Mathematics and Science Study (1999), Boston, Mass., Boston College.

Thrupp, M. (1999) *School Effectiveness: Let's Be Realistic*, Buckingham: Open University.

Van Amelsvoort, H.W.C. (2001) *Reciprocity and Interaction Between Inspection and School Self-evaluation*, Paper delivered at EU Congress on Quality in Education, Karlstat, Sweden (April).

Van der Grift, W. (2000) *Educational Leadership and Academic Achievement in Secondary Education*, Paper at the European Research Association Conference, Edinburgh, September.

Watkins, C. (2001) 'Learning about learning improves performance', NSIN, *Research Matters* 13, 1–8, London: Institute of Education.

Willis, P. (1977) *Learning to Labour; How Working-Class Kids Get Working-Class Jobs*, London: Gower.

Wragg, T. (2001) Unpublished conference keynote address, Breaking Through to Learning Conference, Merchant's Hall, London (26 February).

Index

Italicised page references indicate that some information is given in the form of a figure or table.